Sometime Never

■□■□■□■□■□■□■□■□■□■□■

Wilfred and Mabel.

Sometime . . .
. . . Never

Wilfred Pickles

AUTHOR OF
"BETWEEN YOU AND ME," "PERSONAL CHOICE"

WERNER LAURIE
LONDON

Contents

◼◻◻◻◻◻◻◻◻◻◻◻◻◻◻◻◻◻◻◻◻◻◻◻◻◻◻◻◻◼◻◻◻◻◻◻◻◻◻◻◻◻◻◻◻◻◻◻◻◻◻◻◻◻◼

Acknowledgments

Grateful acknowledgment is made to the following for kind permission to quote the poems and other extracts appearing in this book:

George Allen & Unwin, Ltd. *Lancashire Pride,* by T. Thompson.

Hodder & Stoughton, Ltd. "How to Live on 24 Hours a Day," by Arnold Bennett.

John Lane, The Bodley Head, Ltd. "My Will," by A. C. Benson.

Methuen & Co., Ltd., and Miss Collins. "The Rolling English Road," by G. K. Chesterton, from *The Flying Inn.*

Frederick Muller, Ltd., and Mrs. Ratcliffe. "Yorkshire's Five," by Dorothy Una Ratcliffe, from *Under t' Hawthorn.*

William Heinemann, Ltd. *Delight,* by J. B. Priestley.

Mrs. T. Thompson. *Owd Thatcher,* by T. Thompson.

Grateful acknowledgment is also made for kind permission to reproduce the photographs illustrating this book:

London Essex Newspapers, Ltd. (Top picture facing page 32.)

Graphic Photo Union. (Bottom picture facing page 32.)

Daily Graphic. (Top picture facing page 33.)

Yorkshire Observer. (Top picture facing page 65.)

Doncaster Gazette. (Bottom picture facing page 65.)

Sunday Pictorial. (Top picture facing page 97.)

R.M.S. *Queen Mary.* (Bottom picture facing page 97.)

Deryck M. Whittaker, Photographer, Manchester. (Facing page 129.)

Illustrations

TO
BARNEY COLEHAN

WHO HAS WORKED SO CLOSELY WITH ME
IN MY RADIO PROGRAMME, "HAVE A GO!"
AS A MEMENTO OF A MILLION LAUGHS

DEAR BARNEY,

You know the sort of life we lead, and just how little time we get to ourselves in our round of broadcasts, rehearsals, journeys all over Britain and public appearances.

You know how we long to get away from it all sometimes.

Well, would you believe it, the chance has come. Mabel and I were glancing through our diary today and found that we have twelve blank days. Maybe you remember what that old Yorkshireman said to me when we were doing a programme in the West Riding: "If tha wants to tek a holiday tek it now!" Anyway, that is exactly what we intend to do.

It's going to be a real holiday, too; not on the Riviera or cruising the Mediterranean or staying in "digs" in Adelaide Street, Blackpool, but in our own flat.

Call it a private sit-down strike if you like, but we don't intend to allow anything to stop us putting our feet up and being our own bosses for twenty-four hours a day.

As Arnold Bennett said: "There are twenty-four hours in front of you. You can't borrow any of it. Nobody can take it from you. It's yours to have and to enjoy."

It will not be easy. It will need all that tact and diplomacy you are always talking about. When the telephone rings, Mabel will say I am busy; so if she tries to bluff you, don't take it too seriously! When we have callers, we will go to earth like hibernating hedgehogs and leave things to our secretary. As for the mail—well, if you write Poste Restante, Exeter, it won't find me, because I will be nowhere near. Nor will a personal call to Leighton Buzzard 129 uncover me—but it might surprise somebody in Leighton Buzzard!

I remember how you laughed when the G.I. at Nottingham told us in *Have a Go!* that if his time were his own he would "just lie under a tree." There are no trees in Devonshire Street, but in our window-boxes are some lovely bulbs that Paul Hart sent to us.

While you are slogging among your files, charts, listening figures and telephone calls we will have our slippers on and nobody to disturb the peace—we hope! The Invisible Man and his wife!

You may not believe all this, and I can't say I blame you if you don't, for there have been so many false starts before. An *Alice in Wonderland* idea it may be, but how well those words of Lewis Carroll fit our twelve days:

> *"Will you walk a little faster?"*
> *Said a whiting to a snail,*
> *"There's a porpoise close behind us,*
> *And he's treading on my tail."*

Well, nobody's going to catch our tail this time, not even you. I'll show thee!

Sincerely,

Wilfred & Mabel

□□□

CHAPTER ONE

Monday

OUR PLAN ALMOST WENT WRONG FROM THE START. I WAS lounging, and smoking, in eighteen inches of hot water when the phone started ringing. There was a strong temptation to throw on a bath towel and call off my moments of luxurious idleness in the interest of my curiosity. Mabel, however, had the presence of mind to call: "I'll take it."

I heard her voice without being able to make out what she was saying to the caller. Then, after about a minute, she came to the bathroom.

"Who was it?" I asked.

"H. M. Tennent's," she replied.

Again I had the feeling that I ought to have answered. This firm of theatrical producers probably had some news of the play I had signed-up for in the coming season at Blackpool. Perhaps there were changes in the script? Maybe they had contracted somebody I knew to take part? Or had they an entirely new proposition?

I was on the point of getting out of the bath to find out when Mabel said: "I told him you can't do anything for twelve days as you're up to your neck in it!"

I splashed about a bit to show that I had heard. "Is that all right?" asked Mabel.

"All right," I said. "Fine."

Our holiday had survived the first round. I began to feel rather triumphant, and safe in my cloud of steam. For how long had I promised myself a bath like this—a real soaking that lasted through three refills of hot water? Once more I pulled up the plug, allowed the water-level to fall, and then knocked-on the "hot" tap.

As the temperature rose I recalled those boyhood days

when I made up my mind that sometime I would have a carpet on the bathroom floor. And how often had I wanted to ridicule people who said that the bathroom was no place for carpeting because the dampness rotted the material. I glanced overboard at the red carpet fitted close to the bath, and briefly wondered why no poet had found inspiration in the comfort, or the cold linoleumized discomfort, of a bathroom floor.

That reminded me. I had decided to choose some poems for the next series of broadcasts called *The Pleasure's Mine*, and I had assured Joe Burroughs, that lean and plain-spoken B.B.C. intellectual who can discuss English literature and the latest problems facing the United Nations with equal spirit and authority, that I would have my personal selection ready immediately after my holiday.

I opened the window slightly and looked out over the rooftops between our flat and Broadcasting House. The perspective of horizontal mews and vertical flats was sharpened by the cold sunshine of early spring. It was one of those inviting mornings that make many people want to sing, some to write and others to don shorts and play football. It brought to mind a poem by a writer, for years a favourite of mine, who has had no popular recognition, John Clare:

"Winter is past—the little bee resumes
   Her share of sun and shade, and o'er the lea
 Hums her first hymnings to the flowers' perfumes,
   And wakes a sense of gratefulness in me:
 The little daisy keeps its wonted place;
   Ere March by April gets disarm'd of snow,
 A look of joy opens on its smiling face,
   Turned to that Power that suffers it to blow.
 Ah, pleasant time, as pleasing as you be,
   One still more pleasing Hope reserves for me;
 Where suns, unsetting, one long summer shine,
   Flowers endless bloom, where winter ne'er destroys:
 Oh, may the good man's righteous end be mine,
   That I may witness these unfading joys."

Monday

I have always been fascinated by the story of John Clare, the Northampton peasant who wrote with such sheer delight about the sun and racing clouds, the wind, birds and flowers; who found happiness in the simplest things, yet spent so much of his life in the shadow of madness, despairing and lonely.

Within a few minutes I was digging among his collected works. The lounge was warm and full of the smell of burning logs—one of the unexpected pleasures of a coal shortage. The glass-panelled doors of the bookcase were wide open behind me; and as I began to delve, Mabel came in with the rug she had started making.

Even the impersonal sounds of London traffic from the street below seemed to imply our security from work on this, the first morning of our twelve days' holiday. But Mabel could not resist going through some of the letters that had arrived by the morning post. She was opening one when I came across Clare's "Seasons," in which he describes an early morning in June and writes so delightfully of those "cobwebs" on the hedges as "fairies' dew-wet dresses hung to dry."

"Just listen to this," I said, and read it aloud. She heard me out, and then said: "What about this for writing?" It was a letter, innocently pencilled with an immense effort at composition, by a bonnie lass of Argyll. Here it is, just as it came to me:

> "Dear Wilfred Pickles,
> I herd Daddy tell mummy that you were not going to be on the wirless for vere long. Will you come to Oban please so I can see you. I am six and I like you. I always listen to you I go dancing on Saturday and listen when I come home. When you come to Oban come in summer for it rains in winter. I will take you for waks to all the nice places in Oban and I will take you to the medow where I get all the wild flowers and I will tell you the name of them. I got 4 prize in summer for my bookes of wild flowers and next summer I will try too. I will take you to the Pulpit hill I will take you on the prom. I will take you in a boat. I have a wee

13

brudher his name is Iain he is 3 he is bad at times and
hits me but he will gro better I hope. Will you tell me
when you are to come and I will meet you at the trane
I have oburn hare and a kilt and frekles on my nose in
summer not in winter and brown eyes and red cheeks
and I will wotch for you love from

IRENE XXX
XX"

Even Shelley, surely, never wrote more charmingly to
Harriet; nor Napoleon more endearingly to Josephine. This
wilful young lady had her plans all ready, and how much
more preferable it would be on visiting Oban to be shown
around by her than to be escorted via the municipal building by the sort of people we call leading citizens.

All too often civic pride becomes civic preciousness in
the hands of local celebrities. And ever since *Have a Go!*
became popular I have spent more energy trying to keep up
conversation with mayors and council chairmen than in any
of my microphone meetings with ordinary, unpretentious
folk who couldn't be dull if they tried.

When my brother was about to become Mayor of Halifax
I suggested he ought to avoid doing two things when welcom-
ing visitors to the town. "Never offer to show them the
council chamber," I said, "and never give them the history
of your chain of office." I appreciate the importance and the
great value to the community of local government, the good
that has sprung from civic pride in the past, and all the hard
work that is done without material reward by councillors
and aldermen. But I have been escorted into so many
council chambers that I see them now as chambers not of
debate but of torture. As for chains of office, I am afraid
I can never get exuberantly excited about the names of
those who stooped under their weight untold years ago!

On the question of the conversational capacity of our
mayors I could write solemnly for hours. Some talk about
their predecessors; others about the extra seats they got
installed in the local park; and there are those who wax
boastful about the city, town or village they represent as

if it were their own private enterprise and the people their servants. Perhaps they get dazzled by the glittering gold that bedecks their necks!

One leading citizen I shall always remember did manage to get off the beaten track, but he could find nothing to interest him more than my name. After mentioning a number of Pickleses I never knew existed, he said finally: "Pickles—I wonder if you have any relatives in Hebden Bridge? I once bought a circular saw there, from a man called Pickles."

As he spoke he stroked his chin, and I noticed that he had a finger missing! It caught me off my guard just as he had once been caught off his, and I only just stopped myself from laughing out loud.

Yet there are times when a chief citizen shows a touching loyalty to his community. I had experience of this as a result of a *Have a Go!* broadcast from that eccentric little Cornish village called Mousehole.

There, in the heart of that romantic county where they still believe in ghosties and ghoulies and talk only in respectful whispers of the superstitions that still thrive, I came across a Lancashire woman. She told me she came from Eccles, a smoky factory town I know well, and I replied: "From a mucky hole to Mousehole, eh?"

Two days after the broadcast came an indignant letter from the Mayor of Eccles. He told me of the public parks and playgrounds that gave Eccles its lungs, and even offered to show me round so that I might alter my opinion. But I had no intention of altering my opinion. I wrote back to remind the Mayor: "Where there's muck there's money!"

While I admired his concern for the town, I wondered why so many people in our industrial areas feel ashamed of their sooty kingdoms. From the point of view of public health there are obvious reasons for getting everybody clear of the factories; but there is no reason at all for the widespread notion that Bournemouth is superior to Bolton, or Leamington better than Leigh.

As for Eccles, I know nearly as much about it as I do about Halifax: I know its sprawling flatness, its beehive nature created by the factories that have done so much to help Britain (Bournemouth included) on to her feet in these years of toiling aftermath. I know its mean streets, too; those acres of architectural monstrosities in miniature where so many happy families sit cosily round their glowing hearths while rain beats on their windows and the wet pavements glisten in the light of the gas lamps.

Eccles! Another town of belching chimneys, with a character all its own despite its lack of visible frontiers; a town that merges grimily into Salford; a town to which most of us owe a debt; a town with more claims to fame than its Eccles cakes—those delicious, puffy, sugar-coated buns spattered with currants. Eccles! Rugged, tough, independent as the people it breeds—and magnificently mucky!

There may be some sensitive citizens of Eccles who see their home town differently, just as there were defenders of Halifax who thought I was unfair when I described the part of Halifax where I was born.

In my autobiography, *Between You and Me*, I wrote of Conway Street: ". . . still today a drab thoroughfare, paved with stone setts, its tiny back-to-back houses sheltering so many people that now I wonder how they can find space to move, let alone live individual lives." That brought post-bags of trouble, not only to me but to some Yorkshire newspapers!

What I meant was that people living in districts like that have too little privacy. There are all too many places in the North where the people have to put up with outside lavatories that can be seen by neighbours. And even these kindliest of people love to talk about things like gastro-enteritis!

It reminds me of the two elderly ladies in the Co-op. queue somewhere in Manchester. "How's Mrs. Jackson keepin', luv?" asked one of them.

"Well, she's not so grand," came the reply.

"Oh, what is it?"

"She's got chronic constipation." A pause. "Do you know, I've known her be down at t'closet for an hour and a half."

"Oh, dear. Isn't she takin' anything?"

16

"Well, just lately she's been tekkin' her knittin'!"

Just as my thoughts were wandering up north, the door-bell rang. Our bell, as we live in a first-floor flat, gives us ample warning; callers have twenty-four stairs to climb after ringing.

I remembered that I had arranged to see a twenty-one year old Nottingham lad about his career. He had written to me explaining that he was at London University, believed he had writing talent, and wondered if I could introduce him to any B.B.C. people who might encourage him.

Earnest and rather shy, he came in. He stayed less than twenty minutes, and before he left I gave him the names of several people. I admired him for his modesty and his appreciation of what he still had to learn.

He had none of the impetuous anxiety that distinguishes most of the young people who come to see me or write about their ambitions.

There was one Yorkshire girl whose letter summed-up the philosophy of our eighteen-years-olds in a way that shows how "sweet eighteen" can be anything but dances and the back row of the stalls. Marlene wrote: "I want to be a 'someone,' a 'someone' on whom people will depend and rely. Not someone to make money, money doesn't count when you are helping people or doing something for your country. I want to write books, articles, stories and plays for people to enjoy.

"Life looks to me so very precarious and insecure. I often wonder what I shall be doing in, say, five years' time. Will I be stuck in this office still, having got no further on in life than behind the same old typewriter? My friends and even my family seem faint-hearted when I plan to do great things and to travel abroad and meet hundreds of different types of people."

I wrote to Marlene: "I have heard lots of stories about starving geniuses living in garrets, but I have never met one! John Galsworthy didn't write a line until he was middle-aged. All this adds up to one thing, however trite it may sound, that you just cannot run until you have learned to walk."

I couldn't resist going on to say: "When I was

eighteen . . ." and told Marlene that I was then doing a dull job. When I was eighteen! The year was 1922, and I was a building apprentice in Halifax. How vividly I can see that dark, stone cottage on the fringe of the town where one night I put on a pair of headphones and heard broadcasting for the first time!

Through the crackling interference came the far-off, almost plaintive, voice of the announcer: "This is 2 ZY calling, the Manchester station of the British Broadcast-ing——" I was unimpressed by this miracle that so fascinated the boy who had invited me to his home to listen. As soon as I took the headphones off, he grabbed at them eagerly; and I remember his mother, a widow of about forty, sitting on one of those comfortless, horse-hair chairs near the table and saying: "Of course I don't want to listen. It's a lot of new-fangled nonsense!" She regarded her son for a moment, then looked at me and said: "Our John won't leave it alone. I don't know what the younger generation's coming to!"

The crystal set on which we listened was a gift from the boy's uncle, who had been helping the family out since the death of John's father in France during the war. The follow-ing morning I started telling my workmates all about what I had heard. It was while I was talking that I remembered what old Jack Waller had told me six years earlier. Jack, a labourer, grey-haired and very wise, had turned to me with those strong, trustworthy eyes and said: "The time'll come, lad, when you'll be able to take a little thing out of your pocket and hear people talking miles away."

Perhaps, Jack, in his simple way, foresaw the day of the S O S, of gale warnings to shipping, of all the social and political benefits produced by B.B.C. broadcasting. At any rate, he told me: "It'll do everybody a world of good!"

Another memory of 1922 was the wedding of Princess Mary and Lord Lascelles at Westminster Abbey. I remember reading of the excitement in London; and how unreal one newspaper headline seemed to me. "Feasting and Jocundity Everywhere," it said.

While the ceremony was going on, I was working on alterations to the Turk's Head Inn at Sowerby Bridge, a

typical Pennine "local" approached through a narrow
cobbled passage. Below us, at the rear of the tavern, was the
still, faintly smelling canal with its eiderdown of green sludge.
Until that day I had never even heard of Lord Lascelles,
though I had seen often enough the forbidding iron gates
of Harewood House and vaguely realized that "somebody
important" lived there. I am not sure whether the landlord
treated us to a drink each because he was pleased with our
progress or on account of the Royal wedding.

Over the bar, one or two of the older customers began
to tell stories about the Lascelles family; and I believe it
was there that I heard that the Harewood Arms, the pub in
the village adjoining the Harewood estate, had only a six-day
licence because Lord Harewood was opposed to Sunday
drinking.

Many years later, I was to attend a dinner at which the
guest of honour was the Lord Harewood whose wedding day
it was when I was eighteen.

Tall, erect, with a military bearing, he impressed me as
a likeable personality. He positively twinkled as he told a
story about the parson who would visit the squire's home
for supper each Sunday after evening service.

"Before saying grace he would glance round the table.
If it was a big, hot meal he used to begin, 'Bountiful
Jehovah. . . .' But if it were cold beef, pickles and cheese, his
opening was 'Lord, the least of these Thy mercies!'"

Marlene's letter had set me on a trail of memories. I
wondered who I would have asked for advice in 1922. There
was no widespread radio listening to impress names and personalities on the population of this country; but I recall my
admiration for Sir Frank Benson, the famous Shakespearian
actor. One day I wrote to him and got a reply in which he
promised that if he ever visited Halifax with his touring
company he would have a talk with me.

I was even luckier with Lillah McCarthy, one of the
most regal actresses Britain has ever known. She was in
Halifax to give a poetry-speaking performance in the ornate
and echoing Victoria Hall, and I had persuaded the organizer
of the show to take me round afterwards to meet her.

All through her performance I sat spellbound and silent, awed by her brilliant reading of Thomas Hardy's poems. It must have been a great strain, yet this poised, ageing woman, grey and beautiful, greeted me as if I were the most important visitor she could have wished for. She asked me to recite something for her, and I chose Robert Browning's "My Last Duchess." She sat patiently listening and at the end told me: "You are a beautiful speaker of verse. You ought to go far!"

Only a few days earlier, desperate for an audience, I had recited one of the poems from A. E. Housman's "A Shropshire Lad" to a labourer fifteen feet underground. At the time we were connecting a pipe to the main sewer!

Looking back, I realize that while I was under the spell of the theatre and was trying vainly to write poetry as well as to read it, I was no recluse. My work kept me out of doors and I went regularly to the Wednesday and Saturday meetings of the debating society at the local Sunday School, and the dances they organized there.

What dances they were! Boisterous, noisy, and full of laughter, they brought the old, greystone building to life. The floor-planking was hardly right for the job, but nobody seemed to mind. At every dance one saw the same faces go whirling past in a flurry of Sunday suits and bottom-drawer dresses, while on the hardwood chairs that lined the room the shy ones and the couples too absorbed in themselves sat out.

All the men used to arrive with brown paper parcels firmly tucked under their arms; and in the classroom that served as a cloakroom they opened them on the floor to reveal shoes you could see yourself in. They had black bows across the front and looked somehow unreal against the heavy, cumbersome boots and thick-soled shoes they replaced. I remember how reluctant I was to put mine on for the first time, and how for more than ten minutes I sat watching others arrive, hastily change, straighten their ties and make impatiently for the dance.

Then I noticed that there was someone else holding back. He was a tall, pale lad with a tight-fitting suit; and he kept fumbling with his brown paper wrapping and looking towards the door. "Well, if I look like he does . . .!" The thought spurred me on. I changed into my shiny shoes; then, as nonchalantly as I knew how, strolled deliberately in the direction from which the music came. This show of confidence was dispelled when I came face to face with the dancers. My shoes looked and felt newer than ever. I felt I could never ask any girl to dance. It was then that I spotted Dolly Sharpe, who was tall for her age and sensible enough not to assume that every man was trying to flirt with her.

I plucked up courage, and in a flash we were dancing. Dolly, a good sport with a sense of humour, looked at me rather quizzically and said: "My! You've fairly got your dancing shoes on!"

From that moment I began to enjoy those Sunday School dances. I would rush home to press my suit with a flat iron and clean it with carefully applied strokes of a brush, a ritual that corresponded in most homes with the practice of letting girls make their own dance dresses.

One of the favourite stories in our family at this time—it was told and retold—was of the time when Aunt Lizzie made herself a dress and used rather too many sequins. In fact, she plastered it with them until it looked more like the scales of a fish than a dancing outfit. Even as she tried it on, she lost confidence, but she went in it just the same.

On the way, she confided to another relative of mine: "I feel like something out of the last act of a pantomime!"

Understandingly, her friends said nothing about it; and everything was passing off nicely when, during the lancers, the curate advanced on his line of four and called out loudly: "Oh, Miss Pickles! You're ablaze!"

What I disliked most about certain special dances were the hard-leaded pencils which were attached to the card with thin yellow cord to mark down the names of your partners. I could never do more than make a scratch with them. But the dancing was fresh and healthily uninhibited: Waltzes, lancers and the military two-step had nothing of the purposeful solemnity of the bear-hugging and rapturous wrestling that goes for dancing these days.

We wore white gloves. From what I have seen of the

modern-age dance halls, their patrons ought to be wearing boxing gloves: in their dreary shuffling they look like punch-drunk boxers saying farewell.

With these thoughts tumbling about my mind I walked over to the window and looked down on Devonshire Street. It was at its busiest, with secretaries and typists scurrying busily to their suburbs—and maybe to their dances; taxis making the most of the rush-hour; and a line of cars and a Green Line bus queueing at the signals at the junction with sweeping Portland Place. Overhead, an air liner droned sluggishly towards an airport west of the city.

It was Monday evening, but it might just as easily have been Monday morning with the traffic going the other way. Or Tuesday morning, for that matter. Or Friday. London, ruthlessly efficient in a bureaucratic way, does not know the damp tedium of Monday morning; nor the adventure of Saturday.

Again those lines of Charlotte Brontë skipped through my mind; and with them came a vision of another Halifax, not the mill-town but the place where home on a Monday morning was a cold, unwelcoming steam-trap.

Everything was cold; the day, the house and Sunday's meat that always turned up for dinner. From the cellar came clouds of steam and the sound of the mangle, creaking and clashing as the wooden rollers turned under my mother's control of the big iron wheel.

How unhappy, how miserable I was! There was no escape from washing day! It took the flavour from pudding and poetry in its clammy totality; it was a return to the Dark Ages, and I hated to eat in the half-light of a room in which the windows and the sideboard mirror were glazed into dull subjection.

Charlotte Brontë knew my washing day all right. "As unromantic as Monday morning," she wrote in *Shirley*. If that parson's daughter in bleak, defiant, ghostly Haworth had been brought up differently, that phrase might never have been born. It is also possible that she might have grown up like Shaw, in which case her inspiration could well have been: "Monday morning—bloody awful!"

Monday

Now, for me, a quiet, steamless Monday was nearly over. I'd lounged about all day and I felt better for the rest, fresher in mind but a bit fidgety.

"Stop prowling around," said Mabel from her chair. "Sit down and tell me what we're going to do tomorrow!"

I looked out over Georgian London, across a skyline unscarred by chimneys; then back to the books, the radio, the television set, and Mabel.

"I'll tell you in the morning," I said.

■□

CHAPTER TWO

Tuesday

STRATFORD-ON-AVON WAS GOING FOR ITS MORNING COFFEE as we drove in. Its air of peace was even more noticeable than on our previous visits; and its façade of architectural contrasts ranging from Tudor to pseudo-Tudor and modern seemed to emphasize its character of sturdy permanence.

Everybody, including the housewives with their shopping baskets and the errand boys on their bicycles, fitted into the casualness of the place. Nobody rushed about. There were no flailing briefcases, no cavernous Underground entrances swallowing up hurrying hundreds.

Stratford out of season was more or less as I had imagined it, but more enchanting. For years I had intended to see it without its crowds of sightseers and souvenir hunters; and for years I had planned to take *Have a Go!* there.

In all that time I could never have picked a better day. The idea of driving up to Shakespeare's town came to me when I woke up early and remembered that I had promised to tell Mabel our programme for the day.

We had breakfast at half past seven, left the washing-up, and set off just as the first dairy cart trundled round from Portland Place. On the way up we had talked of the people we knew in Stratford, and recalled the happy three days we had spent in the Vale of Evesham doing a recording for a radio series which, for us, lived up to its title of *Pleasant Journey*.

For the rest of the morning we window-gazed. Mabel, as usual when we leave London, noticed a lot of things she can never find in the big West End stores; and I was overcome by an urge to buy her a present. I told her to wait outside while I went in a shop and asked for a bottle of perfume and some powder. As the assistant was wrapping them up, it dawned on me that I probably had nothing like the thirty-eight and sixpence they cost. I checked up hastily. I had three and fourpence halfpenny. For a second I panicked. Then, with a "Not be a moment!" to the assistant, I rushed to the door and asked Mabel for two pounds, "quickly."

"You're buying me something!" she beamed.

It was the usual story. Never since our marriage have we planned our shares of income: there have been no strict housekeeping budgets, and when she buys me a present for Christmas or my birthday I am often asked for the money. My trouble is that I have none myself at times of crisis when I intend to surprise her with a gift.

We lunched, as planned, at the Mulberry Tree Restaurant. And what a lunch. It was positive proof that even on present-day rations a good cook can produce an appetizing meal. There was *hors d'œuvres* consisting of mussels, smoked salmon, sardines and lettuce; soup with real flavour; roast beef to delight the most fastidious diner, and Yorkshire pudding that tasted as if it had come straight from the kitchen of a dale's cottage.

We so enjoyed it that I asked to be allowed a few words with the chef. He turned out to be a cheerful chap wearing the authentic tall white hat. "I just want to thank you for a very fine meal," I said, speaking slowly so that he would understand me. The chef smiled. "All right, lad! I'll cook thee some tripe next time tha comes!" He came from Manchester not Montmartre!

Our next call was at The Mucky Duck, where hearty Jack Allen was serving beer to a few of the locals. How pleasant it was to find so many real, down-to-earth folk round Jack's bar! I knew it as a place where actors gathered in the summer season; and it was there, shortly after the end of the war, that I came to wonder what made so many actors and actresses talk so loudly in public and so quietly on the stage.

It has always been a cause for disappointment with me that stage folk, who seem so amusing and full of sparkling originality behind the footlights, are so dull and boring in private life. Their conversation is nearly always prosaic, egotistical and sorely wearing, because they will inflict their volubility on any company, quite indiscriminately.

I suppose it is all part of their stock-in-trade, and who can blame these people who live by selling their personalities and their beautiful voices if they make exhibitions of themselves in public. Even Woolworth's and Selfridge's have to lay out their shop windows!

Performers, as I know only too well, have to work hard; most of them are conscientious, and start, at least, with noble aspirations; and I enjoy their company in the theatre when there is a job to be done. But I have never been able to stand much of them off-stage. Their artificiality sets my nerves on edge.

They probably feel the same about the practical, undemonstrative folk who work from nine to five and spend their lives between their homes and offices or factories, except for a fortnight when they go to Blackpool or Bournemouth or on a coach tour of the Continent. If any generalizations about people are correct, one might say there are two types of folks among us: actors and the rest.

This reminds me of the time, many years ago, when a Shakespearian touring company visited Huddersfield. One of the first things they did on arrival was to recruit a number of local lads to play the part of Roman soldiers.

The manager had them costumed, and then tried with increasing desperation to rehearse them. They had no idea. They were alternately complacent and declamatory; they wandered on the stage in their togas, smoking Woodbines; they mocked each other, laughed at the wrong times, and whispered jokes.

Eventually the manager gave it up. Nearly frantic, he hurried round to consult the principal of the company, a great Shakespearian artist. "We can't open tonight with this crowd," he exclaimed.

"I'll come down," he said.

A few minutes later the Romans of Huddersfield were ushered on the stage and were addressed from the front row of the stalls.

"Gentlemen," he implored. "Tonight we are performing Shakespeare's immortal play, *Coriolanus*. You are Roman soldiers. You have returned triumphant. You have conquered Britain. You have ravished Gaul. Ambrosia is your food. Nectar your drink. The fair virgins of Rome await your caresses."

Then he paused, and added: "And you sit there like a lot of schoolgirls drinking cocoa!"

Soon after leaving Jack Allen, Mabel and I were on the stage at the Shakespeare Memorial Theatre, that imposing and beneficent monument where so much useful work is done in spreading British culture throughout the world.

We squatted on carpenters' blocks, listening, as Anthony Quayle outlined his plans for the coming season and the Continental tour his Shakespearian company were to make. Amid the noise of hammering and clanking buckets and the shouts of workmen busy extending the theatre to give it a bigger seating capacity, this exuberant six-footer in his early thirties looked out over the scene and said: "Doesn't it warm your heart to see it?"

He told us it was their practice to open the booking office weeks before the first night. Thousands of pounds had poured in and they were flooded-out with letters from all over the country and abroad. Quayle recalled with delight that one man had sat outside the theatre throughout a cold wintry night to be first in the queue for tickets. He took his own oil stove with him, and when the box office opened he bought 500 seats.

I asked Quayle whether he thought these crowds came to see stars like himself, Michael Redgrave, Diana Wynyard, John Gielgud and Godfrey Tearle. He shook his head. "In my opinion," he said, "it's Shakespeare they're after!"

"We're not such daft people as they seem to think, then," I replied. And, looking at Quayle, I could not help feeling that here was proof enough that high standards and popular success were reconcilable. Thousands of people clamouring to see Shakespeare! I remembered the response to my poetry broadcasts on the Light Programme. For years I had been warned of such a venture: "Leave it alone," advised those

who professed to understand public taste. "Listeners don't
want it. You'll only do yourself harm by trying it!"

Harm, my foot! We gave them Shakespeare, Milton,
Kipling, Chesterton, Wordsworth, Yeats, Thomas Hardy and
Francis Thompson, and the minor poets, too. Out went the
B.B.C.'s researchers; and in came the mail! Both startled the
B.B.C. Millions of ordinary people were not only listening,
but liking what they heard. I had long suspected that the
managers, mechanics, miners and housewives of Britain
would readily accept poetry, or for that matter any art, but
I was not prepared for such a staggering reaction.

Yet how well I remember that wet evening in the early
thirties when I stood at the back of the pit in the Free Trade
Hall in Manchester listening to the Hallé Orchestra.

Next to me, completely enveloped in the music, was a
small, typical Lancashire man. He wore a grease-specked cloth
cap, a brown-and-fawn muffler and a nondescript suit. As the
orchestra went into the last movement of Tchaikowsky's
"Pathétique" Symphony, with its moving interpretation of
utter despair, the little chap glanced round at me, winked
and whispered, "Gradely!"

The success of *The Pleasure's Mine* convinced me that
the B.B.C. had made a big mistake in making poetry the
preserve of the "arty" clique who dwell in a never-never
world sealed off from everyone else. I also realized that much
of the poetry I had included in the programmes was first
brought to my attention by ordinary, unpretentious Lancashire and Yorkshire folk who paid regular visits to the barber.
It was an old weaver in Blackburn who gave my ears a treat
by reciting that gem of mill-town inspiration, "Six o'clock at
Mornin.'" She introduced me to more of these ruggedly
beautiful poems from west of the Pennines, too.

Then there were my experiences up there on Blackstone
Edge, where hardly a man or woman cannot quote from the
works of those great northern writers, Ammon Wrigley and
Samuel Laycock. And the first I heard of "Eawr Sarah's
Getten a Chap" was when an old man of eighty-odd recited
it over a pint in a pub in Oldham.

He chuckled when he had finished and looked at me

with an eye that had taken all humanity into account. "Ee, lad, thar at B.B.C., but tha knows nowt!"

The octogenarian and all the rest of these poetry-lovers in overalls were at one with Anthony Quayle.

Quayle's words came back to me during the afternoon when I met an old friend, a genuine Warwickshire character called Tom Collins, who farms some useful acres in the softly rolling garden of England at Cowhoneybourne. I was telling him of our visit to the Memorial Theatre, when he broke in with: "Did you hear about that silly —— waiting up all night for seats?"

Tom, mischievously good humoured, doused his pipe on a tough boot. He grinned broadly as I said: "Why, Tom, you don't mean to tell me you don't go to the plays!"

"Not me!" he shot back. "I say: Get the season over, roll on winter and let's have the revues back again!" It matters nothing to Tom whether it was Shakespeare or Bacon, or both, who wrote the plays.

Nevertheless, I could not help feeling that Quayle and his company were doing a wonderful job. I wondered how they would be received in Paris and Rome, and for a moment speculated on the chances of joining them. After all, there must be a good deal of satisfaction in helping other peoples to appreciate our art and writers.

My mind went back to that day in Norway in the summer of 1950 when Louise Brown, that brilliant and charming English ballerina, took the most exciting curtain-call I have ever seen. The setting was a story-book one: an open-air theatre, a natural ballet stage, and an audience of thousands perched crescent-like on the rising ground facing the "theatre." There was Louise Brown, bowing, smiling graciously, tears in her eyes, as everyone clapped and cheered her last performance.

This slight figure had gone out from England to teach ballet to the Norwegians; had set the open-air company on its feet, and was now about to return to London.

As the performance ended, the whole company formed a ring round her, and each member dropped flowers at her feet until she was surrounded by about fifty bouquets. Then, in what seemed to be an unending stream, men and women —and children, too—stepped out from the audience and approached her with small bundles of flowers. Their voices came over clearly. "Thank you, Miss Brown, for teaching me to like ballet," they were saying.

Finally came the turn of a group of schoolchildren carrying wild flowers. And there, as a man ran down the hill drawing the huge, flapping curtain across this very touching moment, stood Louise Brown, unable to speak, tears rolling down her cheeks, an ambassador of art who had done her job well.

It was the outstanding memory of our stay in Scandinavia, and one of the many examples we experienced of Norwegian friendliness. I found that most of these wilful, determined people listen regularly to the Light Programme from Britain because their own radio station, Norse Rinsekringkasting, is only on the air for three or four hours a day. Consequently, Mabel and I were never looked on as strangers, from the moment we landed.

Our guide, Mr. Oxnavaard, who used to read the news in Norwegian from London during the war, pointed out a headline in a daily newspaper: "WILFRED PICKLES I OSLO," it read.

"That's just how they would say it i' Oswaldtwistle," I told him.

Mr. Oxnavaard showed us everything, always with a kindly air of modesty and understatement. Grey haired and quiet mannered, he was proud of Oslo, but his eyes twinkled brightest as he took us over the studios of Norse Rinsekringkasting. Efficient, beautifully panelled and well aired, they were more the Palm Court of Grand Hotel of the British radio listeners' imagination than a B.B.C. studio. I wondered whether Sir William Haley had seen them.

What delighted me particularly was to find that so many Norwegian words sounded like bits of our own northern dialect. I happened to mention this to a Norwegian, who promptly grabbed my arm and beckoned me to follow him round a corner, from where he pointed out a huge sign announcing the Olympic Games: "OLYMPIA LAKEN."

Tuesday

How often have I heard people in Halifax say: "Who are t'Town lakin' today?" And how well I remember what an awful meaning "lakin'" was given in the days of depression when it meant being unemployed.

Dialect words, like "gradely" (first-class), "gaumless" (stupid), "clutter" (rubbish), "fratching" (quarrelling), all have their origin in Norwegian. Nor does the similarity between Norwegians and northerners end there: I found a remarkable resemblance in their unruffled temperaments and their brusqueness.

I talked a lot about this and world affairs with Olaf, a wide-shouldered, stocky farmer who wore a vivid lumber-jack shirt. Every time we reached some serious problem, Olaf would shrug his shoulders calmly, as if to say: "Well, it's awkward. The world's in a bad way. But it's no use losing your head about it now!"

We had met Olaf in the little village of Voss. An intimate little place set in a mountain valley, it lives round its railway station, the focal point of local life. At nine-fifty every night the platform gets suddenly busier. Serious-minded business men having a drink in the local solemnly look at their watches, drain their glass and make for the station.

Housewives join the gathering. So do the children, or those who are still up at that time. The occasion is the arrival and departure of the night train to Oslo. People wave excitedly as it steams in; there is a lull; then the waving starts up again as the train pulls out. It is almost like the greeting a football crowd reserves for its team after a win away from home in the cup. At three minutes past ten, just thirteen minutes after the fuss began, the platform is deserted.

The demonstration has nothing to do with personal welcome and farewells. It is a general gesture of spontaneous goodwill. Before we knew what we were doing, we were waving with the rest.

On the way back to our hotel I suggested to Mabel that this must be the place from which the phrase about "watching the trains go by" originates. Our room was large and warm, with French windows that led to a balcony over-

31

looking the lake. From there we could look out to mountains capped with snow even in midsummer. Everything was peaceful, and the people friendly and easy-going, yet something worried me for days. I had an uneasy feeling that there was a piece missing in the jigsaw of life here; something important which I could not place.

Then it came to me. The birds were not singing. And wherever we went in Norway we never heard a sound from them. It was as if they joined the people in a conspiracy to organize a quiet life. Most Norwegians, we found, prefer small communities and avoid crowds as much as possible. One day we found a perky little village of no more than a dozen houses, right off the beaten track and set richly on the secure but adventurous fringe of a miniature Niagara. There was not a murmur except for the sound of the water as it swirled over and down like so many threads of cotton in a loom.

I marvelled at the raw beauty of the place and shuddered at the thought of living there week in, week out for years, with only a few farmers and fishermen as neighbours and an occasional sightseeing tourist to break the steely monotony.

Yet a youngish man with fair hair and the big, capable hands of the agricultural worker laughed when I mentioned this.

"Quiet?" he exclaimed. "Not here!" And he went on to explain that he had "a house in the country where it is really quiet!"

This relatively talkative young man, who would have been regarded as reticent in Britain, gave me a clue to the Norwegian sense of humour, which is very real. Gazing out over the waterfall and the acres of sharply outlined countryside, he started to recall some wartime exploits of the local people; men he had grown up with, some of whom had died resisting the German Army of Occupation.

Just for a moment his eyes flashed as the memories gripped him. He folded his arms and vigorously rubbed the elbow of one. Then he nodded in the direction of a road that ended abruptly at the river's edge. I noticed that another road came to a similar end on the other side.

"It was in the early winter of 1941," he said. "I was not

32

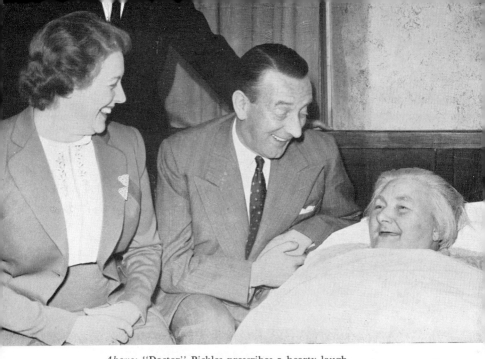

Above: "Doctor" Pickles prescribes a hearty laugh.

Below: A spot of massage before the start of the St. Dunstan's road race.

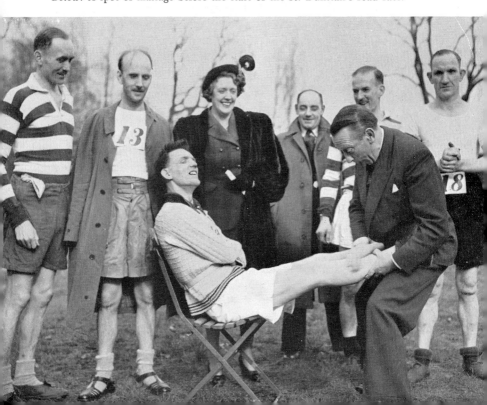

Above: Snap! Wilfred and Mabel entertain two young friends.

Below: Castles in the fire.

here, I am sorry. But the Germans say, 'Build bridge here.' Our people did not argue. We do not like arguing.

"Our men make the bridge and the Germans are very pleased. Our men say nothing. They do not tell that when spring comes and the ice melts the bridge will be swept off and smashed."

I marvelled at the philosophic calm of the man. "And it——" I began.

"Oh, yes, very much," he smiled.

It was another young Norwegian, a citizen of Voss, who kept us enthralled with stories of the Resistance Movement in Norway. He was practising with a rifle on some tin cans about a hundred yards away when we met him. He told us that nearly all Norwegians are marksmen; and to prove it, knocked off one of his targets with no more deliberation or aim-taking than a park attendant spiking litter.

Erik described for us, with characteristic understatement, his life with the underground movement, mostly in the mountains.

Once, the Germans sent fifty bloodhounds after his party; but the sniping was so accurate that not one returned to its kennel.

Erik was no more and no less proud of his country's achievements during the war than most Norwegians we met; and Mabel and I got the impression that the shock of being over-run and the will to fight back that stirred these people must have had something to do with the moulding of their national temperament: sincerity, realism and unselfishness.

How different we found the Swedes! In Stockholm, that capital of mediocre modernity, there was all the evidence of a country with its self-respect gone to seed; a rich country, a country that somehow reminded me of a story I once read about a lad who stayed guzzling cakes in the tuck shop while the others fought a fire at school.

Here was a well-fed nation, with steaks for the asking and cream cakes by the window-full. Yet I found few signs of happiness among the people. Most men and women we met, including the shopkeepers, were sullen and unco-operative.

They showed little interest in us as tourists, and even implied by their manner that they vaguely resented having people from Britain among them. When we went to a dance in the city we were astonished to find that there were more men than girls. The wallflowers all wore trousers. Suddenly, I realized just what the attrition of war had meant to our own country, and what non-participation had done to the Swedes' self-respect and confidence.

How good it was to get back to Norway—"this rocky drama in the ocean," as that great Scandinavian writer, Björnson, called it—and to the people whose natural warmheartedness and love of their fellows gives the visitor a sense of being wanted.

I was still thinking of our holiday in Norway when we pulled up outside the Arden Hotel, Stratford-on-Avon, where Mabel and I usually stay. It is one of those rare hotels where the traveller feels at ease from the moment he arrives. We were used to seeing it full of holiday-makers at the height of the season; now, however, it had an air of restfulness, and the inevitable permanent residents were more in evidence.

There they sat, in the fresh, thick-carpeted lounge, knitting while they watched everything that was going on. I took them to be in their middle seventies, though I am usually so wide of the mark over the ages of old ladies that I might very easily have been ten years out either way.

Both wore ample black dresses and shiny black shoes, and peered over their spectacles at distant objects in much the same way as some bosses do in front of the subordinates. Their needles clicked rhythmically; occasionally there was a pause as one old lady whispered discreetly to the other; and, all in all, they seemed very much part of the establishment.

How often have I seen these quiet old souls in the hotels of Britain, living out their remaining years in this patient, rather frighteningly impersonal way. "One day when I've time," I once told Mabel, "I'd like to study their problem."

Who are they? Why do they live in hotels, where they can have no real privacy except in their bedroom? Every time I come across them I always feel rather sad; for old age seems to me the time when the companionship of relatives and a settled home are most needed.

Yet the majority of these old ladies seem to have money and to be contented. Perhaps my sympathy and concern is wasted, for at least some of them are too self-willed and independent even to want to live with their families. Perhaps, after all, those who live in hotels are the luckier ones, with the economic freedom to choose between staying with their children and leading a life of their own.

I could not keep my eyes off the two old residents at the Arden. I wondered whom they were knitting for, and how much of their needlework they would wear themselves.

Their calm independence reminded me of Mrs. Sullivan, a grand old lady from Lancashire who turned up in my *Have a Go!* programme at Oswaldtwistle. Alert and confident, she was a living reminder that there is fun and laughter even in the eighties of a lifetime.

Mrs. Sullivan had all the unpretentious casualness and candour of the East Lancastrian; her strong, wrinkled hands were as much part of Oswaldtwistle as her voice.

In her grey ruggedness was the whole story of Oswaldtwistle: its industrious past, its mill-hooters; its huddle of weavers' cottages; its bleakness; its flickering gas lamps palely illuminating the wet cobbled streets. Mrs. Sullivan had known it all—the "half-timing," which meant attending both mill and school at an age when she should have been playing rounders or hop-scotch; the unemployment in the dead years when Oswaldtwistle's chimneys stopped smoking; the rattle of heavy clog-irons as weavers went to work on a cold, "muggy" winter's morning.

Yet there she stood, serene as a statue, her hands folded in front of her; a trim figure with grey hair tied in a knot at the back of her head. Not everyone in the public hall had heard of her when she walked on the stage. But they knew her by the time she had finished.

There was no stopping her. She had strong views about the "young 'uns," and the nation's production problems. "There's too much education and too little work being done," she said, adamantly.

That got a heated reception from the audience, a lively crowd of good-humoured folk who are used to outspokenness and provocative viewpoints, even from old ladies of eighty-three! Mrs. Sullivan—I almost called her "Mrs. Oswald-twistle" during the broadcast—put a hand on the microphone stand to steady herself a bit, and told me: "Now don't ask me any questions about history because I know nowt only my own!"

And what a history it turned out to be! This sturdy grandmother started work at the age of ten, and even after the birth of her children she went back to the mill. Now, on her own, she lived in a hilltop cottage just outside Oswald-twistle, and did all her own shopping and housework. I asked her whether she thought the old age pension was enough, and she shot back: "Well, if I can't manage off it, I'll go and get a bit o' supplementary!"

Then came the climax of this astonishing old lady's broadcast. I told her that as she was eighty-three I would ask her about old tunes, and she immediately replied: "Let's have summat I know!"

"What do you know, luv?" I asked.

"'Rose Marie.'"

The tune was struck up. Everybody was laughing, including myself. Then Mrs. Sullivan started to sing. Never have I known an audience change so dramatically from laughter to silent, serious appreciation. It was one of those moments one can never forget. There was not a person in the hall who was not willing Mrs. Sullivan to reach and hold those high notes; and as she sang, so her voice gathered strength. It was a most moving performance. This Lancashire pensioner who had spent her life in dutiful obscurity, was up there, under the spotlight, singing beautifully.

I was lost for words; and after the broadcast I sought out Mrs. Sullivan, shook her hand, and said: "That's the grandest thing I've heard for a long time."

Her eyes danced. She made a gesture of tidying the folds of her dress. Then she replied: "Ee, lad, you should 'ear me when ah'm washin'-up!"

This was not the last I was to hear from her. As the

Oswaldtwistle broadcast went out shortly before Christmas, scores of listeners sent her gifts of money—small sums that would not add up to more than a few pounds.

A few days later a letter reached me. It bore the Oswaldtwistle postmark, and inside was a note: "You have put new life into me! People have been so kind. I enclose £1 for your Invalid and Crippled Children's Fund." Then there was a PS.: "It's been grand. But I'm tired of being on the front row. I've had a back seat all my life, you know!"

Reading it, I somehow felt that *Have a Go!* had done some good in Oswaldtwistle if only to reassure one old lady that the world, as well as her family, was still interested in her. But how many more Mrs. Sullivans were there who would sooner go into exile in hotel rooms than join in the activities of an era in which they felt themselves strangers?

Mabel and I had one other call to make, but as that was on our way back to London we decided to spend a couple of hours in a Stratford cinema where *Trio,* the film of three stories by Somerset Maugham, was showing. We had intended to see it for months, ever since the first reviews, but our wanderings with the *Have a Go!* team had prevented it.

As we had not been to the pictures for something like eight months, it was almost a novel experience; and perhaps it was because I was concentrating so much on the screen that I noticed what I took to be a mistake in the dialogue.

One character, talking about a girl, remarked: "She's pretty, too, and clever as paint!" Afterwards as we drove towards Bretforten through the mellow Warwickshire countryside, Mabel and I argued as to whether this really was a mistake or an intended slip of the tongue. Perhaps we will never know.

• The Fleece, at Bretforten, is one of the loveliest of the old inns of England; the sort of place where you half expect Robin Hood and his Merry Men to turn up in full cry. It is well-beamed and tastefully Tudor, and nestles in the heart of that green and pleasant agricultural and fruit-growing area where only the birds are restless and spring seems to linger longer than anywhere else.

It was just the right time to be in Bretforten when we

arrived, for the sun was setting in a blaze of colour beyond the patchwork of fields, the clouds were motionless, and farm workers were homeward-bound along the lazy roads.

"Every time we get round these parts I feel we should have taken farming up years ago," observed Mabel. I watched the houses and cottages slipping by the car window; cosy homes that were always occupied, unlike the acres of expensive flats in London that hid so much sombre drabness. Here, I thought, is where folk know how to live.

Then The Fleece came into view. I knew just how it would look even before we went in; for we had driven miles out of our way many a time just to spend half an hour there in the company of that most genial of landladies, Lola Taplin. The furniture, carefully kept and well used; the pewter glistening like polished steel, and the oak woodwork sealing the character of the place as firmly as nothing else could.

And there was Lola, jolly, round-faced and bubbling with country tales. As soon as she saw us, she recalled the day when Mabel and I took charge of the bar for half an hour and did a roaring trade serving pints of bitter and gin-and-limes.

"Oi had another B.B.C. man here a short while ago," said Lola, expansively doing a convincing imitation of a man who thinks much of his own importance. "He comes in and says to another man at the bar: 'I understand if I sit here I shall hear some real dialect.'

"My regular customer turns to him and says: 'Doialec! Doialec!—we speak English yere!' "

After a few minutes listening to Lola, Mabel and I reluctantly resumed our journey. Again, this warm, soft countryside wrapped itself around us; and we speculated on what we missed years ago when we cancelled our plans to spend our honeymoon in these parts and went to London instead.

We remembered, too, that family motoring holiday before the war when Mabel's mother walked into a "classy" hotel in Warwick with a chicken under each arm and asked the manager if he could cut them up for us!

"She hasn't changed a bit," I said. Only recently, Mabel's mother, seventy-four and lively as ever, had surprised all of us at a party by singing her annual piece, "Ta-ra-ra-boom-de-ay!"

And she had been the life and soul of the family when we let the New Year in. She joined in heartily when we played like children with a tape recording machine I had bought in Halifax.

Mabel set up the box-shaped contraption in a corner of the flat, switched it on, and then put the microphone in the centre of the hearth. At first, knowing that what we said was being taken down to be used in evidence afterwards, we were rather laboured in conversation. Then we forgot about the microphone as we warmed up on the news from Korea, the meat ration and the new plays in London.

Mabel's mother got on to her favourite topic, her days on the stage in the early years of the twentieth century. It was pure delight, with tales of coquettishness, life behind the footlights, and the behaviour of the audiences. But she was really at her best when talking about the young men who used to chase her—"before I knew your father, of course!"

When she had covered some twenty years of her youth, with encouragement from us, we decided to play back the recording immediately on this humiliating machine.

The voices came out clearly, but Mabel's mother did not recognize her own, so that while we were laughing she was taking it all very seriously. As her voice came out of the loudspeaker, she kept repeating to herself: "Oh yes, perfectly true! That's the gospel!" Her soliloquy was so rich in anecdote and telling observation on an era I had only read about, that I made up my mind to keep the recording and file it away.

Back in London at eight thirty, we put the car away and walked down to the Mason's Arms in Devonshire Street, a breezy little hostel where Weber and Boswell used to call for half a pint of beer. Our luck was in; for there, in a smoke-clouded corner of the bar, was a man whose company is so entertaining I can spend hours listening to his tales.

Ian Mackay, that most brilliant of diarists, whose essays

in the *News Chronicle* have given him the reputation of a twentieth-century Pepys, is a tall, wild-haired, craggy Scot with a delightful brogue and a rich experience of people and their foibles.

Every time we meet I see him in kilt and helmet fighting at Bannockburn. And I have an idea that every time we meet he tries out some forthcoming opus on "the dog"—me.

Within seconds, the voluble Ian was off on a rambling tale, full of names and places and events which his romantic mind glorified and charmed. It was about a minor operation on his eye, "a simple matter, really!" He gave us details, then more, and still more.

"Here it comes," I interrupted. "He's working up to a column!" Three days later it was!

Ian analyses people well, as I know. Once he wrote of me: "He talks about Wilfred Pickles as if he was some other fellow." He is also very precise and logical, two qualities that were evident when he went to Bertram Mills's Circus and worked out how much of her life a girl acrobat spent upside down. Ian based his calculation on a routine of five performances daily.

It was Ian who was so disgusted because nobody in Halifax could tell him where the local "gibbet" was. This amiable man of the world who really enjoys his glass of beer is, to me, one of the giants of journalism.

How well I remember that afternoon when Mabel appeared in *Woman's Hour*. She talked about the difficulties women had in making up their faces in the lavatories of trains travelling at fifty miles an hour; and also mentioned Roger, our amiable mongrel dog. An hour or two later a note was slipped through our letter-box. It had been hastily scribbled.

"Dear Mabel," it said, "congratulations. Thank you for telling us all about lavatories on trains. I am glad Roger got his nose in!" It was signed "Ian."

Time flies when Ian gets going; and being with him reminds me of those lines in "Tam o' Shanter" by Robert Burns:

Tuesday

"When chapman billies leave the street
And drouthy neibors neibors meet;
As market days are wearing late
And folk begin to tak the gate,
While we sit bousing at the nappy,
An' getting fou and unco happy,
We think na on the long Scots miles,
The mosses, waters, claps and stiles,
That lie between us and our hame,
Where sits our sulky, sullen dame
Gathering her brows like gathering storm,
Nursing her wrath to keep it warm."

But Ian had Pat and I had Mabel; and we called it a day.
So Tuesday ended with a journalist; and Wednesday was to
start with one.

CHAPTER THREE

■□

Wednesday

I WAS ONLY HALF AWAKE WHEN THE PHONE STARTED RINGING; and it needed a big effort to leave a warm bed on such a morning. Through the partly opened curtains—we usually draw them at night after switching off the light—I saw a downcast day, grey and forbiddingly cloudy.

From below came the dutiful sounds of early morning traffic and a man whistling on his way to work. I allowed the phone another six rings in case the caller had no urgent business and decided to come through later; and then lost count as Mabel murmured: "Isn't that our telephone?" I feigned sleep for another six rings before the G.P.O. won.

"Yes," I said, wedging the receiver between my chin and shoulder as I fumbled with the cord of my dressing-gown.

A cheerful feminine voice chirped a breezy "Good morning!" and proceeded to tell me that she was writing an article. I might have known! Fleet Street not only never goes to bed, but considers it right and proper that nobody else should, either!

"What I want to know is this," explained the Voice. "Do you like women dressed in red?"

"Yes, so long as it isn't red flannelette," I answered flatly.

"Do you really mean that?" asked the girl in Fleet Street.

"I couldn't be more serious at this moment," I said.

In this conflict of the woman journalist's amazement, and my own mood of resignation, I managed to explain that there is a shade of red which seems to me to suit every woman. "I know what I am talking about because I go with my wife when she buys her clothes," I said.

"In fact I'm going with her this morning to help her choose a coat."

42

And two hours later Mabel and I were in that women's wonderland where the shop floors are carpeted and men in starched white collars explain humourlessly a thousand times a day: "Underwear! Second floor, madame!"

In these imposing palaces of plenty, these battlegrounds where women prove at every sale that whoever called them the gentle sex needed his head testing, there is more for the student of humanity to see than at any circus or cinema. How I love to stand ten stairs above the battle as the bargain-hunters invade the ground floor of one of these department stores!

There is more jockeying for position than at any speed-way meeting; more pushing, pulling, tugging and long-reaching than the rugby spectators see at Headingley or Twickenham; and, in this whirl of flailing handbags and frantic drapery, what man could risk himself? Better to wait at the door—or on the stairs to the second floor, as I do.

From the buzz of remarks one can pick up snatches of conversation, such as one I remember overhearing in a Leeds store.

"I think this'd suit our Florrie, don't you?" A blouse was waved about above the milling headgear.

"Let her buy her own, love. It won't be right if you get it. You know what your Florrie is!"

As Mabel and I pushed our way through the swing doors we noticed there was anything but a rush on. Only a few dozen casual shoppers stalked past the counters.

The starched men were much in evidence, darting authoritatively about like junior officers before a parade. Again I found myself wondering what sort of lives these apparently unbending fellows lead when they are not floor-walking. Do they really dig gardens, and slip into the "local," and play trains with the children? Somehow, I felt they must; yet not for the life of me could I see them doing these things.

"Can I help you, madame?" One of them was speaking to Mabel, and it was all I could do not to burst in and ask him where he lived and whether he had ever worn comic hats and played charades. Did he ever don an open-necked shirt and play cricket on the sands with walking sticks for wickets? And what did he prefer—flirting or playing at darts?

The coat department was almost deserted. A group of salesgirls stood gossiping under a window; and as we passed I heard one saying: "You're not really seeing him, are you, Vi? He's had it! He's forty if he's a minute!"

Through one of the tall, tilted mirrors, I caught sight of the mischievous grins which greeted this observation. It was a rather embarrassing moment for an adjacent forty-six year old; but I felt better when one of the girls detached herself from the party, approached us with an interested smile and asked what sort of a coat Mabel wanted.

I have never felt uncomfortable in women's shops, though I know many men who refuse to venture within fifty yards of them. How often have I followed Mabel, with all the aplomb and dignity of the most experienced floor-walker, through the underwear department, my head in the air, although I admit casting a few sly glances at the corset- and négligée-clothed dummies.

Not for me the long wait outside; I like to pass opinions, to be involved, and I get a real kick out of a little routine I have developed. I ask for a chair, an ashtray and a place of importance. I feel like a Parisian prince of fashion as I cast a pretentious eye over the clothes they produce.

Sometimes I shake my head and exclaim professionally, "No, no, no!" It is the sort of situation that brings out the worst in me, the portentous actor given a chance to play an extravagant rôle. If I carried a walking-stick I would probably thump the floor with it.

This time I was denied a long performance; for the second coat that Mabel tried on seemed just right. The first was a loose-fitting tweed in vast green checks; the sort worn by horsey women at Newmarket.

The salesgirl smiled her triumph; we arranged for the coat to be sent on; and were whisked into the maelstrom of Oxford Street by a bored-looking liftman.

From there we went into half a dozen department stores, as Mabel ferreted out a few odds and ends.

I was quite enjoying the outing; and it occurred to me

that while I would willingly go up fifty floors shopping with her, I had only once bought something for myself in one of these places.

I am easily pleased when I buy socks or shirts and ties; and I don't want to be whisked four floors up for them. I believe this is fairly general among men and may well be the reason for the thriving state of gents' outfitting businesses. I have never been a dressy man, and, but for the wife, I would often find myself at the B.B.C. or on a public platform or at some luncheon wearing outrageous colour schemes.

But I was once an assistant in an outfitting business in Halifax and have never lost interest in the trade.

The one occasion when I did break with practice was during the rationing period when Mabel and I were being entertained to lunch by a London impresario. We were on our way when she noticed that I was wearing a blue tie and a brown suit.

We called in a Bond Street store and the assistant immediately produced a tie I liked. I gave him a pound note.

"Sorry, sir, it's thirty-five and six," he said. This stunned me; but I paid up. Then I asked if I could change my tie in the shop. He beckoned me down the counter and round a corner into a den of mirrors. Then, just as I was leaving, he recognized me.

"Aren't you Wilfred Pickles?" he asked.

I couldn't resist it. I waved the receipt he had given me. "No," I replied, "judging by the price I've paid for this tie, I must be Lord Nuffield."

A few minutes later, on the crowded pavements of Oxford Street, I was recognized again, this time by an old lady from Bradford who a few months earlier had appeared in *Have a Go!* But I saw her first. Who could ever mistake Mrs. Baker? There she was, this sprightly eighty-three year old with the strong grey hair drawn back into a bun over a severe, forthright face; the same Mrs. Baker in the high-buttoned boots who impressed me so much when I met her in Morecambe, and who had looked me straight in the eyes and said gravely: "I hope, young man, you don't go into these public houses and billiard saloons!"

45

Mrs. Baker, who was accompanied by a young relative with whom she was staying for a few days in Catford, looked me up and down for a moment and then shook hands, expressing no more surprise that we should meet in the heart of London on a busy morning than she would if the place had been the shopping street round the corner from her home in Heysham.

It all came back to me, that memorable interview I had with her and how she had told us with touching solemnity of her seventy-one years in the Band of Hope and "her most embarrassing moment" when a man reeled towards her one evening in Bradford, touched his cap with an exaggerated gesture of politeness, and tried to get her into focus.

"You ought to be ashamed of yourself," Mrs. Baker told him.

The man smiled half-apologetically and said: "I don't get like this very often." His eyes softened nostalgically: "And we used to have such good times at the Band of Hope, didn't we? Good afternoon, lady."

After the broadcast she told me a lot more about her life, and as she was leaving she turned at the door, put a warning forefinger up to her face and said: "Remember! Water, pure water, there's nothing like pure water! For health and strength and beauty there's nothing like pure water!"

Often Mabel and I recalled that little cameo as we talked things over by our fireside, and when I started a series of television programmes in which I introduced ordinary folk, Mrs. Baker was one of the first people who came to mind. Calm and unexcitable, she glanced round the studio at Alexandra Palace with an air of forbearance that suggested she had seen much greater wonders in her time; and while some of the other folk I was to interview were still full of wide-eyed curiosity Mrs. Baker produced something from her bag and beckoned me over. It was her Band of Hope certificate. And a little later on, during a break in our preparation for the show, Mrs. Baker showed us what an unquenchable character she is! We had all trooped into a small room across the corridor, where there were sandwiches waiting, not to mention beer, orange squash and gin for those who fancied a drink.

Mrs. Baker took in the alcohol at a glance, and immediately tried to divert everyone's attention from it. "I've brought a little game with me," she said. "It only takes ten minutes. Would you like to play?" It was during this little interlude that Mrs. Baker began to take a grandmotherly interest in the producer of the show, Norman Swallow, a boyish-looking, fair-haired man who has a flair for being well liked. While he was seeing our guests off after the show, she called him aside and whispered the advice she had given to me about the qualities of water.

Her performance on the air was masterly. She looked directly into the cameras and said: "This country is neglecting its Sunday. Remember what the Bible says: 'Six days shalt thou labour!'" It moved Collie Knox to write in the *Daily Mail*: "She looked straight at me and made me hang my head in shame."

The B.B.C. provided a car to take Mrs. Baker to her relative's home in Catford, London. "Just tell the driver where it is, Mrs. Baker, and he'll have you there in no time," I said through the window as she sat expansively in the back seat.

The driver half turned to hear her instructions. She leaned forward confidentially and said: "I don't know exactly where it is, young man, but I'll tell you when we get to the corner of the street!" And Mrs. Baker smiled and waved as a worried-looking driver began their journey into the unknown!

Now, here this morning, was Mrs. Baker again. "You look twenty years younger," I told her.

"None of your bluff," she laughed. "How's Mr. Swallow? Nice young man! I hope he's doing well and will you tell him not to forget what I told him!" I couldn't help smiling as I pictured myself reminding Norman, who hardly ever touches a drink, of the benefits of sticking to water!

I watched Mrs. Baker disappear among the shopping crowds that were already much bigger than when Mabel and I had set out, and wondered what she thought about

47

this London. How often have I met northerners who have told me: "It's a good place to get away from!" I often feel the same way, yet it thrills me to sink into its life, to merge with the hurrying people on its pavements, to hear its busmen and cabbies cursing some unfortunate eight horse-power driver who has got in their way, to see those new-age characters, the "spivs," coaxing women to buy the nylons which they drape temptingly over expert wrists.

I like to take this city's pulse; to smell its fumes on a sharp spring morning when one's nostrils seem more sensitive; to linger at Victoria and watch the trains come and go; to waste time at its Underground bookstalls, dazzled by their clash of colour and their range of magazines and newspapers, some with queer-looking titles like "Oggi." I am insatiably envious of the variety of people of all nationalities and political persuasions and religions and classes and colours who find what they want to read from these magnetic displays.

But perhaps what I enjoy most of all is to be asked by a baffled northerner in the Underground how to get to Euston or King's Cross or the Houses of Parliament. Then I can show off; I can direct him, with great assurance and a northern accent, and the result is that he is either impressed with what I have been able to learn about this awesome metropolis, or he is disgusted that anybody with traces of such a distinctive background as belongs to those born between Derby and Dundee, should own to such traitorous knowledge!

For, whatever he thinks of London, the northerner is inclined to be suspicious and on his guard as soon as he reaches it. He regards it as a paradise for human birds of prey—which, to some extent, it is—and distrusts its loud advertisements, its bowler-hatted business men in pin-stripes, and its bulging briefcases, nearly as much as he does the West End.

It was into this very West End that two Lancashire men came for the Cup Final. They walked into one of the most fashionable restaurants in Mayfair for lunch. They eyed the waiters up and down, stared unbelievingly at the musical sextet playing in the gallery and then noticed the finger-bowls on their table.

"What's these?" asked one of the men. "Is it soup?" The other frowned. "I'll ask him," he said. He wagged a beckoning finger towards a waiter. "Now then, young man, what's the idea of these basins wi' t'watter in?"

Coldly respectful, the waiter replied: "When you have finished your meal, sir, you might care to dip in your fingers and wipe your mouths."

"There y'are," said the questioner to his pal. "Ask a daft question and you'll get a daft answer!"

There were no finger-bowls where Mabel and I went for lunch on this Wednesday. It was one of those landmarks of modern London where so many visitors from the north like to meet, a Corner House. And, as the frock-coated waiter showed us to our place in a recess of the table-packed floor, I speculated about his private life in much the same way as I had done earlier about the floor-walkers.

It struck me that this man with the well-greased hair and pale face had probably never walked home with muddy shoes and his arms full of bluebells! It made me feel rather sad; for this waiter, all waiters, are the fallen idols of what was once for me a grand illusion.

As a boy in Halifax I used to regard them as symbols of a frighteningly attractive world of millionaires and society women in which men lit cigars with five-pound notes and the women were glazed with diamonds. Waiters were part of this extravagant dream: they knew all about this world and its people; they were informed, aloof, experienced.

I was still in awe of these men right up to my wedding day when something happened that shattered every fantastic notion I cherished about them. Mabel and I were dining in a London restaurant where the food was excellent and the service like something out of an Arabian Nights scene. Our waiter had a halo! Then, only a few minutes later, as we were on our way out, I noticed a room door slightly ajar. I had to take a look—and almost instantly regretted my curiosity. For there, rubbing away at a cruet and standing amid an array of dining-room silverware, was a waiter in his shirtsleeves. I saw his starched false shirtfront; and, what was worse, his striped shirt.

This was perhaps my first experience of the inescapable truth that growing up and getting about have a price and that too many peeps behind the scenes are apt to strip away much of life's glamour and gay mystery. I felt this especially when I played in pantomime at Leeds. All the glittering spectacle was reduced to buttons and bows and tape measures and stop-watch precision until what had begun as an adventure had become as "unromantic as Monday morning."

There is a story about Tennyson which aptly sums up disillusion. A woman who worshipped him as a literary idol was in full spate of praise when the poet looked hard at her and said: "Your corsets are creaking!" She blushed and did not reply.

Then, after a long pause, he added: "I'm sorry, madam! It's not your corsets, it's my braces!"

One of my most vivid disappointments in life is the loss of that magical vision of the London theatres I once enjoyed. Names like the Playhouse, the Apollo, the Garrick, all meant something great and colourful and inaccessible; romantic, wondrous places that were always in the daily papers and where famous actors and actresses were to be found. Now I know only too well, how Joe, Fred and Harry pull the strings; and I no longer have the impression that greatness lurks behind every dressing-room door; in fact, I am quite certain it doesn't.

It was while I was thinking of these things that I realized Mabel and I had not been to a London theatre for months, except on business. "What about doing a show tonight?" I said.

"Oh, yes!" She looked down the West End theatre advertisements in the *Evening News,* jabbed emphatically at the Ambassadors Theatre and said: "That's where I'd like to go!"

It proved a sound choice. The play, *Lace on her Petticoat,* was so moving and so well acted that I immediately phoned a telegram of congratulations to the cast, saying: "A grand play brilliantly acted. Thank you for a very pleasant evening."

What delighted us more than anything was the quality of two very young actresses who were getting their first chance in the West End, Perlita Neilson and Eleanor McCready. During the interval, I said to Mabel: "What a shame the place isn't full!" There were empty seats all over the theatre, whole blocks left vacant by the cost-of-living index. Outside were other signs of the slump in show business and the luxury trades: no queueing for cinemas and theatres, lifeless pubs and taxis plying eagerly for hire.

As we strolled towards Leicester Square a taxi slowed down as it drew alongside and a voice called "Taxi, sir?" It was the first time this had happened to us since before the war. I shook my head and, turning to the wife, said: "I didn't think it was as bad as that!"

And I remembered those blacked-out wartime years when I almost had to plead with taxi-drivers for a journey; and that summer evening in the flying-bomb days when one driver grudgingly picked me up and was openly scornful when I gave him a half-crown tip on a five shillings fare. As I put the change from a ten-shilling note in my back pocket he leaned out of his cab, slammed the door I was just about to close, and muttered something about American generosity. His behaviour so annoyed me that I warned him: "The time will come when you will stand in a rank shouting 'Taxi!'" He pulled away and across Marylebone High Street towards a group of American soldiers.

Now my hasty prophecy seemed to have been proved right; yet I felt some sympathy for the cabbies; for they do a nerve-wracking job of real value to the city. I wondered why they should have to be so dependent on the tipping system, which I have always disliked. In our travels up and down Britain, Mabel and I have found hotels where it is customary to spray the staff with pound notes, and at one, prominently displayed in the foyer, was a notice which read: "Have you left anything?" A Manchester man with two briefcases and an umbrella glanced at it and commented sharply: "Should be: 'Have you anything left?'"

Walking under the glare of the neon signs and the dazzle from the cinemas, pin-table saloons and those chromium corridors where young men in broad jackets and loud ties sip coffees with their Americanized girl friends, I thought for a moment of the men down the pit at Brodsworth and Atherton. They would be on the night shift now in that black underworld that is so much cleaner than London's.

No coffee and cakes down there! No tips either! How fantastically unbalanced life seemed! Here, in this unsettling world of gaudy pleasure, were hundreds, probably thousands, who had come to expect tips from tourists and night-outers, for services that seemed superficial and unskilled, and undeserving, when compared with those of the miner.

As we turned off Leicester Square we noticed two shifty-looking men on the kerb waving magazines under the noses of passers-by. Pulp magazines with "Paris pictures": they seemed appropriate enough in this demoralizing district where so many young people spend so much time pretending to be happy.

We passed a theatre where men elbowed each other to look at the "stills" of undressed women; and I remembered what an old friend of mine from Bolton had said about this same display. "They'll see nowt they can't see at home," he exclaimed.

In the entrance to another theatre was a placard that screamed in red and black scrawl: "Revolting? Or Ferociously Exciting?" A few yards away, the ugly posters had this message: "It's Dynamite. Terrifyingly Real!" The diseased carcase of the West End came out in more of these sores of theatrical superlatives as we went along: "Suspense Galore!"; "She Loved Them—Then Killed Them!"; "Yours To Thrill To!" Here was Broadway all over again, with all its sensationalism and extremes, with its draped young men and film-struck, over-made-up girls, in platform heels and Woolworth jewellery.

When I was in America there was nothing I hated more than Broadway; but this London impersonation was as crudely nauseating as jokes about lunacy. Mabel seemed to sense what I was thinking; perhaps she was sharing my reactions to all this squalid gaiety. "Let's get a taxi home," she said. I nodded.

A little man held up three magazines, and I caught sight of the words: "Secrets of Freemasonry." Two tall young men with wavy hair and flashy bow ties and brown and white shoes flopped over each other in helpless laughter at some hidden joke, and a string of girls who could be no more than eighteen or nineteen passed haughtily by, leaving scent on the air and young men on the scent.

I looked up at Garrick's statue, now more than ever a lonely sentry on a field of desecration, and wondered what David Garrick would think today if he could only see this surrealist nightmare of twentieth-century escapism all around him. David Garrick, perhaps the greatest of British actors, who did so much to bring dignity and honour to the stage and to raise standards in the theatre!

I looked at Mabel. "I'm no Sunday School prude," I said, "but. . . ."

"All these girls would be a lot better off out of it," she said.

"Lending a hand down at St. Dunstan's Club in Marylebone Road, for instance," I added.

They passed us in droves, young girls attracted by the bright lights but who were yet on the right side of our law and the popular conceptions of morality. If only they could be shown where they are needed, and where they can learn to enjoy themselves healthily instead of wasting their lives on the helter-skelter pavements of Leicester Square and Piccadilly Circus!

A taxi pulled in just ahead of us and we waited while the passenger alighted. From a nearby foyer a commissionaire had come forward to open the door for him, and as we got in he held on to the handle, peering at us expectantly. I'm blowed if I'm going to give him anything, I thought.

He held on. The driver turned round impatiently. "Would you mind shutting the door?" I called. The commissionaire did as I asked, but he banged it so hard that it nearly came off its hinges.

As Broadcasting House came in sight I remembered that

somebody had telephoned some days ago to say there was a parcel for me, so we decided to leave the taxi there and walk the few hundred yards to our home.

The huge, curving building looked deceptively deserted, but I had hardly finished assuring Mabel, "Straight in and out! No shop-talk!" when I spotted two familiar faces.

John Snagge and Frank Phillips were just going off duty, and Frank, the announcer who never stops talking even when he is miles from a microphone, was obviously involved in a long discourse which he broke off abruptly to greet us. Then he got going on another topic—cricket!

Frank talked away fifty-to-the-dozen and, when John got a word in, it was to say: "I think it would be a good idea to put Wilfred up for membership of the club, don't you?"

It turned out to be a new club at Lord's for cricket enthusiasts, and both John and Frank were members. Frank, who is tall and wears horn-rimmed spectacles, and looks like what a schoolmaster ought to be, eyed me up and down analytically and said: "I suppose, as a Yorkshireman, you are eligible?"

"For heaven's sake," John pleaded with me, "tell him that one about Lancashire and Yorkshire!"

Mabel smiled, as if to say that if this wasn't shop-talk it was a busman's holiday! But the audience could not have been better for a cricketing tale: two English gentlemen who invariably remind me so strongly of the characters portrayed by Basil Radford and Naunton Wayne that I never think of John Snagge and Frank Phillips without linking them with Continental trains and a film scene in which two Englishmen in a serious scrape in Nazi Germany could find nothing more to worry about than the Test Match score!

I told them of the time when Jack Ikin was batting for Lancashire against the bowling of Bill Bowes in one of those traditionally keen Roses' games. Suddenly, during a very quiet over, the ball did a peculiar trick: it rose sharply and skimmed the bails. Slowly, the right-hand bail trickled off its pedestal and fell to the ground. Ikin, that stylish batsman who is also a humorist, stooped, picked up the bail and re-placed it. Then he gazed steadfastly into the eyes of Wood,

54

the Yorkshire stumper, and said with a bland smile: "Windy, isn't it?"

"Ay," retorted the brusque Wood. "Mind it doesn't blow thi bloody cap off on t'way to t'pavilion!"

This story so delighted Frank that he began to speak in praise of the cricketing qualities of the two great northern counties; and he had the anecdotes, as he always has, to make what he said worth hearing. Only once have I known this great talker silenced, and that was at Bath, where we had met by accident at the same hotel.

I was doing *Have a Go!* in a village near this lovely spa town, and Frank was there to introduce the Russian conductor, Nicolai Malko, to a concert audience. After our respective shows we met over dinner, and in next to no time Malko and I had found common ground on almost everything that was mentioned. We talked about music and people and Lancashire and Yorkshire and Continental holidays and the B.B.C. It went on for two hours, though it seemed like two minutes.

Malko, a volatile, grey-haired man, with flashing eyes and a charmingly explosive manner, immediately impressed me as one of those rare personalities who are richly endowed with a taste for life. He even entertained us all with twenty minutes of conjuring tricks. As we left the dining-room, he stage-whispered in attractive broken English: "I am afraid we talk too much! One man in ze partee he was ver silent."

"That was me," said Frank Phillips.

"No, no, there was another," insisted Malko.

Phillips laughed. "Oh, you mean Barney!"

The little conductor's eyes sparkled mischievously. "He give 'em the money, eh—but he give no conversation!"

This developed into one of those nonsensical private jokes that will probably go on interminably; whenever Barney Colehan opens his mouth, either Mabel or I can be expected to tease him with: "He give no conversation, eh!"

When we left John Snagge and Frank Phillips in the half-light of a fuel-saving city, they were still talking about cricket. There was a nip in the air, and across the skyline was a daub of orange-red, a tempting invitation to tomorrow.

55

All the way down the broad stretch of Portland Place the homeward-bound headlights shone like crude glow-worms; a policeman strolled slowly past us; and in the gutter was the wreckage of a day, the crumpled headlines about Korea and Four-Power Conferences, and. births, marriages and deaths.

For a few moments I wondered what it all meant. Here, in this fussy little world of good and bad, but mostly good people, there seemed no third dimension; only a flat, super-ficial layer of hopeless activity that made me feel as insignificant as an ant on an ammunition dump.

In one of those taxis passing by there might be a scientist capable of disposing of half a million people by the touch of a switch. I glanced over my shoulder at the looming shape of the Voice of Britain in a troubled world. The lights that burned in Broadcasting House seemed to stand for all that was worth while in the struggle for men's minds. It was a reminder that the science of cynicism had not beaten man-kind, and that while people were free to reason and to talk among themselves there was always hope.

Inside the flat I opened my parcel, marked "Urgent," and while I was unwrapping the two layers of brown paper and the fold of cardboard with all the eager anticipation of a seven-year-old at Christmas, I reached the last wrapping of tissue. It was sealed by a sticky paper band on which had been written: "A token of thanks for the pleasure you gave me with your poetry programmes.—W. S., Plymouth."

And inside I found a beautifully bound book. It was the Oxford Book of English Verse, and the craftsmanship of the bookbinder was worthy of the writing. I fondled it tenderly. My thoughts went back thirty-two years to a late afternoon in Halifax. I was fourteen and passionately devoted to poetry. I badly wanted the Oxford Book of English Verse and I could not see how I would ever have enough money to get it.

I searched the shelves of the Halifax Public Library and found the book, and stayed there for twenty minutes in a sort of trance as I explored it. Then, on an impulse, it was under my coat. I hardly dared look the girl librarian in the face as I presented another book to have the date of return stamped on the inside of the cover, and for a moment I almost retreated back to the shelves to return the stolen treasure.

The girl's antiseptic cleanliness and neat, well-manicured hands seemed to emphasize the shabbiness of my own dishonesty. She flicked the book open, pressed the stamp on it, collected my card and, as she returned the book to me, she smiled: "It's a very good one," she said warmly. I felt ashamed, for I did not even know what the book was called or who had written it. It was only an alibi.

For weeks I knew the nagging remorse of one who has fallen below his own standards, but I was afraid and reluctant to return the plunder that gave me so much pleasure.

As the memories came flooding back of occasions when I feared that somebody might discover it in my drawer, I suddenly realized that I probably still had the book. In a moment I was rummaging among a pile of books in the bedroom. And there it was! Faded, its leaves tinged with the brown of the years and the thread of its binding stretched loose so that the front cover almost came away, it was at once a source of happiness and regret.

I took it in the kitchen to show Mabel. I hardly noticed the smell of frying bacon. When I had told her the story, she said: "Well, perhaps if you hadn't 'borrowed' that book you would never have done *The Pleasure's Mine*—and a lot of folk would have missed hearing poetry."

After supper I went to the bookcase, took down my own leather-bound copy of the Oxford Book of English Verse and began wrapping it up. I carefully put the tissue round the volume, then the cardboard, then the two layers of brown paper. And on the outside I wrote in big letters:

The Chief Librarian,
Halifax Public Library,
Halifax, Yorkshire.

CHAPTER FOUR

□□□

Thursday

Mabel brought in the morning papers for me to read in bed. There they were, arrayed on the eiderdown, those familiar and ever-welcome titles: the *Daily Express, Daily Herald, Daily Mail, Daily Mirror, News Chronicle, Daily Telegraph, Daily Graphic* and *Manchester Guardian.*

Every day for years I have read them all; for I have in large measure that bump of neighbourly curiosity which makes the British the world's best when it comes to newspaper reading.

I am not sure whether this diet of sensation and scrambled egg and serials with my cereals is a good or bad thing: all I know for certain is that I cannot get on without it. Fleet Street often makes my day just as it sometimes mars it. Some stories anger me; there are editorials that make me fume against the leader-writers, and cheap circulation-raisers like photographs of partly dressed chorus girls usually persuade me to throw the offending paper into a corner before I have got beyond the front page. But that happens on Sundays more than on weekdays.

I enjoy reading the humorists, the sports commentators (these are just as likely to enrage me as are the political correspondents and radio critics!) and the gossip-writers. There is nothing I read more eagerly than paragraphs about people: the comings and goings of the Royal Family, the way the latest arrival from Hollywood has "sold" himself at the previous day's Press conference in his honour, the fantastic hobby of some politician in the news, or Mrs. Jones's reaction when she took over the five hundredth postwar house at Hogmarsh-on-the-Wold. Give me this chatter first, then let me see the headlines on the United Nations or the row in Parliament and the latest forecast about income tax changes. How well I remember a newspaper feature that used to hold me spellbound before the war: "These Names Make News" it was called—and how readable it was!

With the record of yesterday—its successes and tragedies, joys and sorrows, hope and despair—strewn across the bed, I was just getting round to the back pages of sport when the phone rang. For a second, without reason, I feared it was bad news. Either Mabel's mother or mine was ill, or perhaps our bank manager had decided to draw a line on our overdraft.

"It's the vicar of St. John's, somewhere—I didn't quite catch the name," Mabel called.

The vicar's voice was rather timid and hesitant. "Oh, Mr. Pickles," he began, "we're having our garden fête in July —the fourteenth—and I wrote to you three days ago asking if you would be so good as to perform the opening ceremony."

"I'm afraid I haven't got round to it," I said.

"Never mind," said the vicar. "Anyway, I just thought I'd tell you that we had a meeting of our committee last night and it was unanimous—well—er . . . with one dissension— that you should be invited!"

For once I knew precisely where I would be on a future date; and on the fourteenth of July I was appearing in a play at Blackpool. As I tried to apologize with the hope that I might be invited another time, I was overcome with a longing to know who the dissenter was! What was he like? Was he old or young? And what was his job?

This unknown odd man out so tickled my imagination that I told the vicar: "I'll bet he gets things done on that committee of yours!" There was a cautious cough from the other end, so I shut up. But afterwards I gave Mabel my impression of what he was like; I stood behind a chair, gripping its back as I worked up a fine peroration about the arrangements for the garden fête.

Then I strode defiantly across the room where I thumped the table and boomed: "If the women of this parish aren't capable of making trifles and jellies on their own without having to call in outside caterers, then it's time we gave the job up!" The Church militant here on earth!

Mabel laughed. I followed her into the kitchen. "What's the programme for today?" she asked. "Don't forget we are having lunch at the House of Commons. I've got a few things to tidy up before we go, so you can go out till then." I decided to take up a month's-old invitation from Arthur Christiansen, editor of the *Daily Express,* to attend his editorial conference. We had met him at Clacton, where I had been invited to open a trade exhibition and, as a "local," he was there with his wife Brenda.

I sensed the high-voltage of the man, his energy and virility and drive, the moment we shook hands. What also impressed me was his modesty and that mild objective assurance that so often draws attention to personal qualities much more emphatically than hours of self-praise. I suppose this surprised me a little, for I had come to think of the editor of the *Daily Express* as a remote and dark power in the land, a worldly deity dangling strings from his glass-and-chromium tower with the leading people in politics, administration, radio, the Arts, sport and society as his puppets. From the contents of his paper I knew he must be no respecter of persons, and I hardly anticipated the amiable, uncynical man I found him to be.

We were to learn a good deal more about him a few weeks later when we spent a most pleasant evening at his house at Holland-on-Sea. He and his wife are one of the happiest married couples I have ever known, and this solid, simple domesticity helps the visitor to feel comfortable and at ease. How well I remember that hectic Saturday night as we played "crap," the American dice game, into the small hours. There was "Chris," as they all know him in Fleet Street, from proprietors to copy-boys, kneeling on the carpet and holding the dice up to his mouth as he pleaded with them to fall right.

To me he appeared the supreme example of the family man; no harsh and heartless editor of the Hollywood pattern here, but one who was remarkably efficient and knew how to relax and how to leave his work at the office.

Mabel was in the midst of one of her sudden spasms of turning out the cupboards when I left, and I found Arthur

Christiansen's office no less hectic. One after the other, carrying newspapers and folders, the executives of the *Express* trooped in. They all looked alert and rather anxious. From the jig-saw of these men's ideas, I thought, would be shaped the paper that more than four million people would buy the following morning.

There were no polite preliminaries. Arthur Christiansen, it was plain, was no mere papier-mâché editor, no nominal ruler of this phenomenal news-gathering organization; he was very much the boss, almost terrifyingly efficient behind the sort of desk a prime minister would be proud of, and he was instantly in command.

Why, he wanted to know, had another morning paper carried a better picture than the *Express* that day of some event in the news? Why had a reporter not gone out to the Riviera?

Gradually, the slight tension eased as plans for the following day came up. Here were men, whose names had been only by-lines to me, putting in more ideas and work in a few minutes than I had ever dreamt went into the entire production of a newspaper. The experience of nosing-in on newspapermen's affairs, as a change from having them nose-in on mine, was delicious. I was revelling in it. Then, out of the blue, Chris caught me unready: "Any ideas, Wilfred?" he asked with a grin.

"It's time somebody wrote a feature about you," I said.

Then, the humour gone, he was ordering a man to be flown immediately to Rome—as if it were a town in the Home Counties; and was provisionally placing what material was already at hand in its position in the paper. He spoke of page four with the same reverent solemnity as might be reserved for the thirteenth chapter of Corinthians. His grasp of the situation and ready assessment of news values astonished me. Ideas, suggestions and synopses of articles and reports seemed to fly in on him from all directions, and I was quite thunderstruck to see him fielding them like an expert cricketer in the slips.

I wondered how he ever found time to help the smaller papers, the local weeklies for which he has a well-known regard. Many an editor with a weekly net sale of under twenty thousand copies owes much to the editor of the *Daily Express*, not only for advice, but for stories.

When I mentioned this after the conference, Christiansen just laughed. "I'm a reporter from Wallasey, remember!" Here was one of the few men I had ever met who was so big he could afford to play himself down, whose achievement was all the more notable because he had led his paper to the top in the most competitive business in Britain without once resorting to the sex-and-vice pattern that has brought some papers their mammoth circulations. Politically, the *Express* is a law unto itself, but its wholesome policy does it great credit. We talked over this question of newspaper standards for ten minutes. "Write for the women," Chris said, "and the men will follow you!"

On the way back to the flat to pick Mabel up, I thought of that other popular editor of the day, Percy Cudlipp, of the *Daily Herald*. Like Christiansen, he seemed an integral part of this street of a million stories, where the traffic is so tight that I have stood for twenty minutes waiting for a chance to cross, where reporters and photographers can be seen frantically hailing taxis, and where the man on the opposite stool in the milk bar might well be a new Boswell and the stranger buying a paper a second Chesterton.

How many of the young folk walking past at this very moment, I mused, are young journalists from the provinces; awed, enchanted and a little frightened by the atmosphere of this fabulous street. And what are their chances of ever getting to the top? I noted the City-dressed gentlemen in their bowlers and black suits and with their inevitable umbrellas, and wondered whether the sight of these totally unrepresentative people was enough to make hardworking youngsters shy from London life? I guessed not, for wasn't Fleet Street full of men like Christiansen and Cudlipp, who had climbed all the way, not on a rope of old school ties, but via the footholds they had so diligently carved themselves?

The hustling democracy of the place reminded me of the story Percy Cudlipp told me of his own election as a member of the exclusive Garrick Club. He had invited me there to lunch one day, and as I sampled its plush, leathery serenity, he said quietly, in that high-pitched, toneful Welsh voice of his: "Let's sit down and I'll tell you why I like it so much."

Percy, broad, rather pale and for all the world like a prizefighter with an intellect, then explained that at the time he was put up for membership he was editor of the *Evening Standard*; but when the committee met, he had left to become editor of the Labour *Daily Herald*, a change that worried one or two Colonel Blimps. They went round the club asking members, especially the two who had submitted his name: "Is this fellah all right, do you think, old boy?"

"Anyway," said Percy, "they had me—and we're all great friends."

Opposite us, as we talked about Britain and South Wales and the miners, sat that unique actor, Alastair Sim, his face as radiant and entertaining as a June morning at Land's End. I soon found that Percy Cudlipp was the sort of man you can be frank with, and we were still at the soup stage when I said rather provocatively: "You know, the depression and misery of the people isn't real. It's only in the newspapers!"

"That sounds all right," he retorted.

"I've proved it!" I shot back. "In *Have a Go!* I've proved it!"

He brightened. "Well, if you're so sure about it, why don't you go out into the country and find this spirit of the people—and write about it, for us? Nothing political in it. Straightforward stuff, you know. Write about the people as you find them."

I liked Percy Cudlipp. I jumped at this chance, not only to prove my point, but to look a bit deeper into the lives of the ordinary folk than *Have a Go!* had allowed me to do.

In less than three weeks I was on my way, with the back seat of the car full of maps and reference books about geography and local history and facts and figures about unemployment and the cost-of-living and production.

As we set off, Mabel looked at me rather quizzically. "They'll make a politician of you yet, Pickles," she warned jokingly; she always addresses me by our surname when she is in that mood.

But I felt then, as I still feel today, that when one has built up public confidence in one sphere it would be taking an unfair advantage to make political use of it. I have my views as a voter, but I am not temperamentally fitted to be a loyal party man, and I believe strongly that I have a duty, during an election, not to try to influence people who may happen to like me as a radio artist. If democracy is to mean anything at all, it must be kept clean and more sincere than some of the noisier politicians would like, and this means that well-known actors and singers and sportsmen, and other non-political personalities, morally have less right (in the interests of unemotional voting) to shout their heads off on polling day than their admirers and listeners.

This was the sort of formula I was working out in my mind as we struck north east for Ipswich and Yarmouth, our first answer to Percy Cudlipp's challenge. I recalled that we had only been to Ipswich once before and on that occasion Mabel sprained her ankle; yet, on arrival, it seemed an inviting, familiar place, a country market town distinguished not only for its great historical associations with King John and Cardinal Wolsey, but also for its cattle market.

I was soon talking to the locals, to Matthew Wood, a sixty-six year old farmer with a grey moustache, bright eyes and one of the heartiest laughs I have ever reeled from; to Skipper Bill Polley and his mate Jim Cook on the motor-barge *Gladys* in Ipswich Docks; and a score of other men and women who all had stories worth hearing.

Then we made our way to the Gainsborough Housing Estate, picked a house at random and were greeted, as I wrote in my first *Herald* article, by "a smartly dressed young woman, Mrs. Doris Churchyard, holding in her arms eight-months-old Robert, as bonny a sunburned lad as you could meet in a day's march."

The rest of the family were Jack, her husband, Audrey, aged twelve, and Sheila, aged eight. They were just going to start their tea when I got there, but they didn't mind the interruption. Jack is a metal-pourer at Ransome, Sims and

Above: The Christmas party in a Dr. Barnardo's Home.

Below: Brothers in Arms. Wilfred, suitably attired, greets his brother Arthur, the Mayor of Halifax.

Above: **On Ilkla Moor baht 'at! (But no point in being "baht coat" as well.)**

Below: **Lunch with the miners. Has the blushing victim on Wilfred's right just been asked "are yer coortin?"**

Jeffreys, one of the biggest makers of agricultural machinery in the world.

His job is to pour out the molten metal into the moulds, and he is continually splashed with hot metal so that his clothes are full of holes. He was wearing a green and yellow pullover that was like a colander. He is thirty-two, was in the Territorials and fought throughout the war; he came through Dunkirk, went in again at Algiers, fought through North Africa and Italy, finishing up in Vienna. . . .

I asked Jack if he was contented with life and he said: "I have a good wife and a happy family, a job with good money and a house at eleven and eight a week, including rates; there's a pub nearby and two good schools for the kids. For the first time in our lives we've had a holiday this year —a caravan at Clacton. So what more could anybody want?" What, indeed! Here was a real, happy man. I wish there were more people like Jack and Doris in the world.

There was the spirit I had mentioned to Percy Cudlipp. And a point of view that would presumably suit his paper. But Bill Polley saw things rather differently. When I asked this sturdily independent young man if things were better than before the war, he shook his head: "No," he said, "ten-bob notes are harder to come by and they only buy a quarter as much." I wondered what the policy makers on the *Herald* would think of that! Either way, I seemed to be winning, for even Bill confided that he wouldn't change his job for anything in the world. And the article appeared just as I had written it.

So the journey went on, covering Coventry, Tyneside, Hull, the South Wales Valleys, the Black Country, the Potteries, Sheffield, the Yorkshire Dales, Lancashire, Glasgow and Edinburgh. We saw Britain at work, at play, and in her home; we met the housewives during the shopping rush and the men at their machines; we talked, with the setting sun as our lighting effect, to a young shepherdess in the Dales and to the folk in the shadow of the Gorbals. At Tunstall, one of the Five Towns made famous by Arnold Bennett, a place with its sleeves up and a smoke-pall to testify to its

Sometime Never

activity, I ran into a white-haired old lady with a jolly face
and a mind of her own.

She was walking sedately along with a shopping basket
full of fruit and groceries linked on her arm. I stopped her
and asked her who she was, a question that was received
with such an inquiring look as to compel me to tell her my
name first. Still puzzled, she shook her head, but volunteered
she was Mrs. Elizabeth Oakes and was eighty-six years old.

"Never heard of me, luv?" I coaxed.

Again she shook her lovely white head.

"Haven't you got a wireless?"

"Yes, I often listen," she said tolerantly.

"*Have a Go!*—Wilfred Pickles—never 'eard 'im?" I
asked more anxiously.

Once more it was no. "Never mind," she exclaimed,
"even if I don't know yer, have a biscuit, young man?"

She opened a bag and I took one, munching it as we
walked along talking about this wonderful woman's life: she
had mothered ten children of whom eight were alive, and
when I questioned her about grandchildren, she chuckled
and her eyes glittered: "Don't ask me, young man, I can't
count 'em!"

A brave woman, independent beyond imagination, she
had been a widow for thirty years and now lived alone,
doing all her own shopping, cleaning and cooking.

"What's your recipe for keeping so active?" I asked her.

She became confidential. "Well, listen, young man. I
have a pint of bitter beer with me supper every night of me
life and if you take my advice you will do the same!"

It was easy to write articles about people like Mrs. Oakes.
Percy Cudlipp was pleased with the way things turned out,
and so was I. But there was one blot on these pages of news-
print which upset and annoyed me. Up in the Yorkshire
dales we had come across two Newcastle girls on a camping
holiday, both nineteen and only a few months out of school.
We discussed the beauty of this part of the world and how
good it was to be alive, and then I asked one of them, the
darker of the two, what she would do if she had the power
to change something. She pondered for a moment, as she

66

knotted and unknotted her headscarf, and then replied: "I would change all Communists into Conservatives."

I reported this in my article, but it was left out, the only deletion in the whole series. I thought it was a sign of weakness; it was niggling, unwarranted and unforgivable, and I wondered what sort of people some of our editors and subeditors and so-called policy makers take us for.

With these thoughts racing through my mind, I got back to the flat. Mabel was ready and we set out right away for the House of Commons. Soon we were in that part of London which always sends a thrill of pride through me: the area around Trafalgar Square and Whitehall, with its architecture that is as sturdy and reliable as Big Ben, and almost as full of historic significance.

Outside the House a thin line of people struggled alongside the railings waiting for their chance to go in. The policeman on the door examined our passes with the air of one who has an important part to play in our Parliamentary democracy, and then we were inside, through St. Stephen's Hall and into the Central Lobby, where M.P.s and their visitors were grouped about.

There was something satisfying and reassuring about it all, an atmosphere of calm continuity and of genuine citizenship. It was there in the woodwork, it was there in the person of the policeman who every few seconds held up a green card and called out the name of some visitor, while the M.P. who had been brought from the Chamber stood alongside, vaguely trying to pick out his caller, and it was there in the explanatory gestures of one Member who was having difficulty with four earnest young people, presumably his constituents.

We had not been there more than half a minute when a stocky, prematurely greying young man, dapper and mild-mannered, approached us with his hand outstretched. And, as Harold Wilson and his wife and Mabel and I made for the dining-room, I thought back to that soggy summer's day in Knowsley Park, Liverpool, only a few months earlier, when we had met this brilliant Yorkshireman who, at thirty-four, was President of the Board of Trade, and had Britain's economic welfare in his hands.

It had poured down for days, but the United Nations Rally which I was opening and at which Harold Wilson was the main speaker was held just the same.

Open-air events like this, especially when they are in the middle of a morass of mud, can dampen the ardour of most folk; but not the United Nations supporters who flowed in their thousands over the churned-up acres of parkland. The rain streamed down their faces and from their capes and hoods; the sky was black with promise of hours of deluge; but they came and stayed.

Cars could not get near, and when Harold Wilson's saloon was bogged down a photographer snatched a picture which duly appeared in one paper with the caption: "Labour Party in the Mire Again!"

It was one of those occasions when there is no time to feel sorry for yourself because you are too busy seeing others immeasurably worse off: the pathetic figures of the rose queens or beauty queens troubled me a lot. There they all were, their crowns and sceptres splashed and their hair swamped out of place and hanging dejectedly down drenched faces. But they could still smile and were anything but crestfallen.

We had our lunch—cold beef, bread and butter, tea and trifle—in a draughty marquee that was being flapped about noisily by the wind. It was then that Harold Wilson suggested that we might like to have lunch at the House sometime—"in rather warmer surroundings."

He meant it literally; but now that I was inside this wonderful building the warmth was round the heart, and what surprised me was that even M.P.s could take it all for granted, as some of them seemed to be doing. The dining-room was a-buzz with conversation, as might be expected when so many talkers gather together. For some reason we got on to the fuel situation and Mabel came out with a forthright suggestion. "Why don't you get some nylons and sewing machines and washing machines into the mining areas?" she asked Harold Wilson.

"Washing machines I might manage," he said. "But nylons—I'm absolutely sunk. I only wish we could!" During this lunch we also met one of the most entertaining men I have ever known—that little Lancastrian with the permanent glint of mischief in his eyes, George Tomlinson. How often had I heard people say, "How can a half-timer be Minister of Education?"

But, by his work and devotion to the job, George Tomlinson won the respect and admiration even of his critics. Dressed sedately in a morning suit, looking rather older and greyer than I remembered having seen him in his days at Rishton, where he was secretary of the local Weavers' Association, he was nevertheless the same wittily eloquent character with the goblin-like quality that instantly wins the confidence of those round him.

I always think of George Tomlinson as one of the real success stories of our day, the one man I know who can teach Dale Carnegie how to win friends and influence people. In that attractive Lancashire accent he has managed to preserve through years of association with dons and diplomats, he was soon off on one of his cotton-town tales. It was about a mill-owner who decided to have a clock erected on top of the mill building.

At seven o'clock one morning he discovered his foreman standing in the yard with his watch out, staring at the clock.

"What're yer doin', Joe?" asked the boss.

"Ah'm waitin' for t'clock to get up to seven afore I blow t'whistle," replied the disgruntled foreman.

"Dammit, Joe, don't be daft! I allus set t'clock by thy whistle!"

George Tomlinson rested his knuckles on his hips, leaned slightly backwards and said: "I wor up i' thi 'ome town t'other week. Thi brother were t'chairman and when I told 'em a tale thi brother nudged me and said: 'Hey! That's one of our Wilfred's!'"

"What did YOU say?" asked Harold Wilson.

"I said, 'Ah know it is, but I 'ave to get educated!'" What a man!

As we were leaving the House, there was a sudden rustle of interest. Mr. Churchill had arrived! There he was, his grim, determined figure weaving forward like a human landship; his lips set firm and his eyes full of battle. I knew that this was a moment I would always remember, a flash of history; for here was a leader who would be talked about by future generations.

He was as much a part of the Parliamentary pageant as the Thames, that "liquid history flowing by." He was part of the lasting glory of this great city; and I could only think how petty and unfortunate were political labels against the backcloth of London.

I recalled the last time I had been seized by this love of our capital city. It was when we went to the Tower of London to do *Have a Go!* After the recording, the Chief Warder, splendid in his scarlet uniform and black hat with its ribbon of red, white and blue, asked us if we would like to see the Ceremony of the Keys.

With the swirling mist of a winter night sweeping up from the Thames behind us, we stood in the echoing, cobbled road near the Bloody Tower shivering but excited as a tiny party of men appeared in the haze. We heard a gate shut; the metallic precision of marching guardsmen, and the rattling of the keys.

The Middle Tower was locked; then the Byward Tower; there were crisp commands in the distance; then, by the light of the swinging lamp carried by one of the guardsmen, one could pick out the drab grey of their uniforms, the blazing scarlet of the Chief Warder's, and the timeless shade of the masonry at the Tower's gates. There was a flash of steel as a sentry smacked to attention.

Then the steady left-right, left-right of the advancing party that was history on the march. "This," whispered one of the residents of the Tower, "has gone on night after night for centuries. Nothing stops it, not even wars and bombing!"

It knocked me silent. It was one of the most humbling moments I have ever known. In the cold half-light there was a sudden challenge: "Halt! Who goes there?"

"The keys."

"Whose keys?"

"King George's keys!"

Standing before the night guard, the Chief Warder raised

his hat and called "God preserve King George!" "Amen" came the answer.

The voices were strong and sure.

High on the steps overlooking the ceremony, a lone bugler began the "Last Post." Just as its last spine-chilling note died away, the hour of ten started to strike. Such is the precision of this event that its climax and ten o'clock coincide perfectly, always.

Presently, the Chief Warder moved forward and up a line of steps into a central tower, where the keys were locked away. And there Arthur Henry Cooke, the Chief Warder whose picture in colour has appeared all over the world as a tourist inducement, told me with quiet pride of some of the tradition of the Tower. He was part of it himself, this ex-soldier with the finely chiselled face and a row of medal ribbons that included the M.M. and D.C.M.

He loved every moment of his unique job of locking everything up. I was so stunned by the occasion, so much under the spell of this seemingly immortal business, that I unwittingly came out with what must be one of the most foolish things even the Beefeaters have heard.

With the entire ceremony over, I looked hopefully at Mr. Arthur Henry Cooke and said, "Can I see the Crown Jewels?"

Yes, I said it just as simply as that; for all the world like a child who knocks on your door and says, "Please can I have a drink of water?"

As I had been watching them get locked up securely behind portcullises and sentries, amid rifles and bayonets and shouted orders, and officers-of-the-guard, for the past ten or fifteen minutes, it must have seemed quite fantastic to Mr. Cooke.

But he remained calmly unruffled and, with only a glimmer of a smile touching his mouth, said, "Could you come at ten thirty in the morning?"

When we arrived home, Mabel said: "Could I see the Crown Jewels! Was your face red!" This was not a question, but a provocation.

"It always is," I said.

71

"You'd better never ask a Beefeater for his most embarrassing moment. He might say 'When Pickles came. . . .'"

"All right," I said. "I slipped up."

"Slipped!" Mabel exclaimed. "You were nearly beheaded!"

That did it. The floodgate of fun opened up. We laughed ourselves to sleep.

■□

CHAPTER FIVE

Friday

OVER BREAKFAST WE GLANCED THROUGH THE MORNING'S mail. As usual, we made for the parcels first: there were three of them, all small. In one were cigars, which I never smoke; the second contained a box of chocolates, while the third was a book with the high-sounding title, *What's Funny—And Why!*

As I thumbed through it, Mabel tugged at the sleeve of my dressing-gown and said with a wink: "Somebody evidently thinks you ought to know."

"This," I said, "is something I feel strongly about. I don't want to know why anything is funny. It spoils the fun. It's like me telling you a story and then having to explain it. And anyway, what's funny to some people isn't a bit amusing to others."

"It can be just the opposite," said Mabel. "Do you remember the time we did *Have a Go!* at the Royal Mint?"

I remembered all right. There they all were, hundreds of happy workers enjoying the sight of their mates appearing at the microphone. It was such a wonderfully spirited audience that I felt comfortable and easy and uninhibited on the stage. I came out quite spontaneously with a gag which I might have hesitated to use on other occasions. "This," I said, "is the only nationalised industry that is making money."

The men and women for whom coinage is a legitimate business seemed to think it was funny. But, hearing the broadcast in their homes, a lot of sensitive folk were upset because they thought I was "getting at the Government." Postcards came to me by the score; the B.B.C. had a big mail on the matter, too—and some listeners started splashing the

Party paints around in letters to the newspapers. I was quite satisfied that the joke was funny—and therefore legitimate—and I had a clear conscience about it when I asked myself whether I would have come out with a gag about nationalised industry, private enterprise, or, for that matter, co-partnership, if there had been a Conservative or Liberal Government at Westminster.

But this joke and its aftermath reminded me that usually you can't amuse all the people all the time with any one joke. It seemed futile to start trying to analyse the reasons for things being funny or objectionable. All that seemed to matter was that some topics tickled people at certain times, and that the British people had a capacity for poking fun at their own troubles.

How clearly some of our wartime humour stands out in retrospect. It was part of our armour; it rattled our enemies and consoled the strained and nervous folk among us. Even at the time of Dunkirk, probably our darkest crisis in the whole six years, we were telling tall stories about the Home Guard; and, during the Battle of Britain, I remember hearing in a Manchester club about the Spitfire pilot who, as he drifted down on the end of a parachute, saw a woman coming up towards him.

"Have you seen my Spitfire going down?" he yelled. And back came the reply: "No, I haven't, young man. Have you seen my gas cooker going up?" Who in the world can say why that is funny?

It is even harder to take Robb Wilton's fun to pieces for scientific analysis. Yet the inimitable Robb—what a gift he is to this country!—had the nation roaring with laughter during those years of desperate anxiety and peril. Who will ever forget the cautiously protesting henpecked voice plaintively coming out of the loudspeaker with those memorable words that sum up an unforgettable milestone in the lives of most of us: "The wife said to me—'What're you doin' to help?' And I said: 'Doing? I'm guarding England.' She said: 'You are?' I said: 'Well, there's me . . . and Fred Ingham . . . and Jack Smith!'"

What a great craftsman, what a master of timing a gag!

I recalled Robb Wilton's words of inspiration for Mabel and we laughed again at the memory. Then Mabel reminded me of the time when Robb Wilton and I were introduced from the same platform by a mayor.

Portentously, and with the air of one who knows, he glanced in turn at Robb and myself and then announced us as "two of the most famous names in Britain—household words—names every child in the street knows!" And he concluded: "On my left, ladies and gentlemen, is Wilfred Wilton and on my right the one and only Robb Pickles!"

Robb and I glanced across at each other and burst out laughing with the rest of the people there. Then, very astutely and with the sharpness of the born humorist, Robb piped up with: "As the Town Clerk has just told you——" The rest was drowned in a renewed outburst of laughter as His Worship protested: "Nay, nay, lad—I'm t'Mayor!"

How can anybody start to analyse such inspiration? It was just a matter of a dropped brick thrown back with an exaggerated gesture. It was a clash of pretentious and easy-going personalities. It was a case of people in the public eye taken down a peg in front of their own folk; not that this is always funny.

Two of my most amusing experiences have arisen from what some sensitive souls would regard as personal slights. Once, as a spectator at a Test Match at Old Trafford, I was suddenly surrounded by a brawl of boys with autograph books. There they were, pushing, craning, stretching out their arms with books and pencils on offer. I had signed four or five when, just as quickly as they had come, the boys disappeared. I was left on my own, except for a very impatient-looking third-former whose book was in my hands. I looked up, noticed the smiles on the faces of the grown-ups who had seen what was happening, and then spotted the counter-attraction. There, in the midst of a milling mass of school caps and blazers, was the face of Denis Compton.

He grinned and shrugged his shoulders in resignation. The incident genuinely tickled me; and for weeks afterwards I saw those eager, fickle youngsters and Denis Compton's smile, and I wondered what sort of expression I had worn at the time.

Then there was the occasion when I was told a man was waiting for me in a classroom of the north-country school where we had just recorded *Have a Go!* When I went round to meet him, he pushed back his cloth cap that was almost threadbare at the rim, stroked a stubbly chin thoughtfully and, slowly shaking his head, said: "Are you the feller I've been listening to all these years?"

He moved back slightly to get me into focus. "Well, by gum!" he exclaimed. "You're not what I expected. You're such a little 'un! Anyway, you keep goin', lad—'cause when television comes up 'ere, tha's had it!"

He was not being offensive; only frank, as so many Lancashire and Yorkshire folk are. Nor did he think what he said was at all the sort of thing that makes people laugh; yet it set me going until I was almost bursting, and whenever I have told the story to friends in different parts of the country they have found it almost as entertaining as I did.

This was undoubtedly one of my most embarrassing moments; but why it is funny is just as mysterious as the reason for the laughter-raising properties of the answers to my questions about embarrassing moments. I remember once discussing this topic with that grand artist, Douglas Byng. We were not going into why things are funny so much as what things are funny; and "Duggie" recalled the time when he was playing in pantomime and was advised one morning that all the workers from a local firm of lawn-mower manufacturers would be in the theatre that night. As, in pantomime, there is a time-honoured custom of introducing gags to suit parties who have taken large blocks of seats, "Duggie" thought out a fresh "piece" for his act.

"When I was out with my lawn mower this morning——" he began. But he told me: "There was dead silence." In the wings he asked somebody what was wrong, only to learn that the lawn-mower firm's outing was not fixed until the following night. It had the effect of finally convincing me that the border-line between what is funny and what is painful, tedious or offensive is often hard to define;

and once we are tempted into the maze of speculation and examination of what makes people laugh we are on the way to losing our sense of humour altogether by so guilelessly trying to make a science of something so complicated and unpredictable as human personality.

I often recall a story told me years ago by J. B. Priestley which always makes me chuckle. Yet it is simple, straightforward and true, and all the better for telling in Priestley's gruff, pouting, almost affronted manner. I was in Leeds at the time, and we were talking about plays and pantomimes and home life when he mentioned that he and his wife had taken on a new cook-housekeeper and her husband.

Priestley stuffed a plug of tobacco firmly into the well-burned bowl of his pipe, struck a match and held it aflame as he went on: "We-ell, as you know, whenever you get a man-and-wife team like this, one always works better than the other. But we made him into a butler and togged him out in a tail coat one evening when we had some friends coming."

Just a hint of a grin creased Priestley's face. Everything had gone well, it seems, until the new butler asked one of the guests: "Would you like a sweet?"

"No, thanks, I prefer cheese!"

The butler held his ground, hesitating. "Aye, that's the trouble," he said. "You see, we're not very flush for cheese."

Ever since I first met Priestley, and for years before that as an insatiable reader of his novels, I have admired him. I like his blunt forthrightness, his courage and sincerity in sticking to honestly held opinions that may be unpopular and which may be used against him. I have known him difficult and rather pompous at times, but he is soon restored to favour when I pick up one of his articles or essays.

One day Mabel and I went to his home on the Isle of Wight, saw his farm and his old manor house and the writing retreat he designed like the bridge of the *Queen Mary*. Nearly all the time we were in his company this Yorkshireman with a natural endowment for seeing beauty in words, did the talking. His mind is ranging and penetrating; and he does not easily leave a subject before he has entertainingly made the most of it.

It has always struck me as rather odd that Priestley, who is so interested in people, should be subject to spells of boredom. I remember one lunchtime in Manchester when several of us from the B.B.C. had got together for a drink at a pub in Piccadilly. Priestley, I think, was there to do one of his famous *Postscripts*.

Suddenly he noticed that one young producer, John Cheatle, was buying drinks for a second time. "Cheatle," he called brusquely. "You're throwing your money around, aren't you?"

Cheatle, a poet with a talent amounting almost to genius —he died in tragic circumstances during the war—turned from the bar and waved his hand to dismiss the point. But Priestley was not to be denied. "No, Cheatle, not again!"

John laughed and said: "Oh, it's all right. Expenses and all that! 'To entertaining Mr. Priestley . . . !'" There was a spasm of laughter from the rest which died on their lips as Priestley frowned and said in a tone of sullen sombreness: "But I'm not being entertained!"

There was another incident involving this unpredictable man and the B.B.C. in Manchester. It was at a time when he was going to the studios fairly regularly and it was the corporation's practice to detail somebody to look after him during his stay. Once, a rather dreary B.B.C. official in the traditional mould of bureaucratically unimaginative correctness got the job. I have never heard what happened, but the following day Priestley made his displeasure plain to the B.B.C. "Never send that man to look after me again!" he boomed. "He told me his life story, then he told it all over again—and then he started to tell me what he had just told me!"

The rank or station of people never worries this courageous battler and I have always cherished an imaginary picture of the way he told Ogilvie, who was at the time Director-General of the B.B.C., what he thought of a situation in which the head of the nation's broadcasting monopoly had not even got an official car. It rankled with him; and he laid the law down about it with so much force and common sense that the director-general and other chief officials got their cars.

Priestley had never thought much of the circuitous ways of officialdom, just as he is inclined to scorn the pin-striped proprieties of the over-cautious public servant. He has found plenty of scope to exercise these dislikes at the B.B.C. He would not spare Sir William Haley's feelings if the director-general were to talk with him on the subject of British broadcasting!

Yet, for all his great and powerful qualities, I always see in him the ambitious boy who has got on through his own talents and intends that everyone should recognize this fact.

I am sure the next two stories are quite untrue, but at least they are amusing. One was supposed to have happened at a London ceremony where famous people were rolling up every few moments. Two girls, wide-eyed and excited, were busy celebrity-spotting, when one of them picked out Priestley's bulky figure on the steps.

She pointed towards him. "It's . . .!"

"No, it isn't!" retorted her friend, knowing what name was going to follow.

"But it is, I'm sure!" insisted the first girl.

Priestley sensed their uncertainty. He passed them, then walked back the way he had come in, stopped in front of them and said brusquely: "I am!" I like the story, too, of the literary sycophant who gushingly approached him at a party with: "Oh, Mr. Priestley, I think *Angel Pavement* is the most wonderful thing that's ever been written!"

He fixed his admirer with a glare. "Is that so? What's the matter with *The Good Companions*?" Despite this aggressive, glowering exterior, Priestley is a sensitive man with a talent for putting thoughts and feelings into simple, easily understandable language; and I have always envied his writing ability. One of his recent books, *Delight*, gave me great pleasure. It was packed with essays; personal, everyday experiences that happen to most of us, but which we lose in the moment of their occurrence.

One of Priestley's openings is so delightful a piece of writing that I quote it often: "When I am playing with small children (and I am an old and cunning hand) I do all those things that bore or irritate me in my adult life. For example,

79

I plunge, to their delight and mine, into ritual and tradition, create secret societies, arrange elaborate ceremonies of initiation, invent mysterious codes and passwords, turn Freemason, Oddfellow, Rosicrucian, member of the Illuminati."

Thinking of Priestley, I went over to the bookcase where I keep so many of his works and took down *Delight*. I turned to essay thirty-seven and read it aloud to Mabel—not for the first time. In it, Priestley shows another side of his nature, the prank-playing schoolboy who delights in frightening senior civil servants. Who but Priestley could write this: "This may seem a cruel sport, sadistic delight; but there is some excuse for me, if not for you, because I am the kind of man nearly all civil servants dislike on sight; and, indeed, some of them dislike me, I gather, even without seeing me. To work, then. First, select your man, preferably one who, if he does not make a mistake, is about to be promoted or given a title; and then outline to him, with plenty of rhetoric and some magnificent gestures, a huge, crazy scheme that will not only involve his department but also tangle him up with half a dozen other departments. Hint that some very influential personages are already enthusiastic about this scheme, but mention no names. Sweep away, like the rubbish they are, his objections. Enlarge grandly upon one of the unsoundest details of the scheme.

"Then when he protests with more vigour, suddenly change your tactics. Banish all smiles, large gestures, warmly enthusiastic tones. Become the coldly hostile intriguer. Stare at him as long as you and he can bear it. When you speak again, be careful to mention his name and, if possible, his official position. 'So, Mr. Clibtree,' you say sourly, 'as assistant secretary in charge of Snarks and Boojums in the Ministry of Jabberwocky, you are entirely opposed to this scheme, are you?' Then nod several times, make an entry in a pocketbook, mutter something about the Press and Questions in the House, declare in a louder tone that you are busy, already late for a more important engagement, give him a last grim smile and march straight out. Delightful? Perhaps not."

Mabel and I were still talking about Priestley when the phone rang. It was Fred Fairclough, of Wigan, who is our friend and accountant. His first words were: "I've got some bad news. . . ." I could see his reason for warning me; but on the other hand I probably felt more upset than I would have been if Fred had come on and said outright that Tommy Thompson had died.

It was the short of shock that unnerves you. I felt suddenly sad, dispirited and at a loss. "What is it?" Mabel asked anxiously.

"Tommy," I said. It was all I could say. It was enough; for although it was only a few weeks ago that we had done a programme together in the North, one of his *Under the Barber's Pole* sketches, full of Lancashire humour and mill-town irony and understatement, Mabel and I had wondered for months how much longer he could go on. Tommy Thompson was seventy-one, the last of a line of great and undervalued Lancashire writers. As Fred went on talking, I heard nothing. My mind was too full of pictures of incidents involving Tommy—in his native Bury; in the Manchester studios, and in his own modest "semi" with his family around him.

That last show we had done together came back fresh in all its detail, and I remembered a moving passage he quoted in his script which now seemed to have even more meaning:

"Lay a garland on my hearse
Of the dismal yew;
Maidens, willow branches bear
Say I died true.

My love was false
But I was firm
From my hour of birth;
Upon my buried body lie
Lightly, gentle earth."

What a man this Tommy was! And what a writer! He dug out the riches of Lancashire character in all their unpolished splendour, and concentrated them into writings that must endure. He not only flattered me by saying he enjoyed my interpretation of his work, but wrote a character for me called Owd Thatcher, a scoundrel, a ne'er-de-weel who would not work, but a man with a great philosophy, for all that.

For years Owd Thatcher had had his say on the Northern air, and even in these moments of sadness, when somebody very close had gone for good, I chuckled at the echo of those never-to-be-forgotten words that Tommy put into Owd Thatcher's mouth: "Work! Ah leaves it to them as wants it! There's got to be workers an' gate-sitters. Ah'm a born gate-sitter. Everybody falls into one class or t'other; and you can tell t'gate-sitters when they're born. They need less powder than their more unfortunate brethren!"

Tommy, a bulky six-footer who began his working life as a half-timer in a cotton mill, was not conscious of his wit. He had none of the chromium sophistication of the B.B.C. literary set—in his own words, the pavement was his university—but there were few radio writers who could not sit at his feet and learn. Brought up in the harsh, rough-and-ready atmosphere of the cobbled backstreets, he made of his surroundings not a penance but an education. It was a schooling that kept him free from the filing-cabinet mentality of so many modern writers who classify and categorize humanity. Everyone he met was a thrill to Tommy, who was such an enemy of textbook routine that he never put a carbon paper in his typewriter. More than once, B.B.C. producers tactfully suggested that it might be better to make a copy. Tommy would nod his approval, but would continue in the way he had always followed. It was an attitude that worried the B.B.C. men who feared that one day his script would be lost in the post, and lost irretrievably.

During rehearsals he would often roar his head off as we acted his script, for he was not at all convinced that he had written it. Nevertheless, he was quick to seize on shortcomings in the sketches and, in his own way, was something of a perfectionist. I remember when Alick Hayes, a producer who had won a reputation for his national shows on the Light Programme, was transferred to Manchester and given *Under the Barber's Pole* to handle.

After one rather ragged run-through, in which he had

to intervene several times, occasionally in conflict with
Tommy, he smiled and explained: "I warned you when I
came to start working with you that I'm an awkward ——."

"I don't care what sort of —— you are," retorted Tommy
flatly. "It's this 'ere script I'm bothered about!"

There were many people who thought Tommy vulgar.
Nothing pleased him more than to hear this said of his work;
for he was at one with the Prayer Book in his belief that
when something is written in the vulgar tongue it is written
in a language that people can understand. And when there
was criticism of the vulgarity of dialect, Tommy's pride rode
high on a Lancashire accent.

He saw the punch and forthrightness in dialect; he
sensed the poetry just as he sensed the music in the clatter
of clogs, and he rebelled against the idea of using soft words
for what he regarded as better, honest-to-goodness, vulgar
ones. It had the effect of a scratched gramophone record on
a sensitive conductor to call a nightgown slumberwear in his
hearing. And a pregnant woman was in the family way, not
"an interesting condition."

There was pink, embarrassed reproof in the eyes of a
few people in the studio one night when we ran through a
Thompson script which had a scene depicting Owd Thatcher
with a boil on his behind. And this is how Tommy made
the old rascal describe it: "Th'owd woman gave me a plaster
to stick on it. So I bent mysel' down in front of t'wardrobe
mirror—an' befoor I knew where I were, I'd wapped it on
t'wardrobe!"

And the man who could write such dialogue was also
capable of expressing his regard to dialect in terms so chal-
lenging and scholarly that Manchester University awarded
him an honorary M.A. degree. Once, in the studios in Manchester, a girl of fifteen was brought in and introduced to
Tommy. He smiled at her, reassuringly and with a benign,
comforting gesture that was meant to make her feel at ease
in the strange surroundings. He called me over and introduced me.

He explained that the little girl wanted some advice
about dialect. "If you want to speak it, luv, then speak it

and be proud of it. If you don't want to, then leave it alone. It's nobody's business but your own." He paused for a second. Then he added: "But I think Chaucer would have been much more at home in Lancashire than within the sound of Bow Bells. After all, he did call shoes 'shoen,' as we still do in Lancashire."

But many a time this surprising man emphasized to me that he would prefer to let the dialect die a natural death than have it preserved artificially, like folk-dancing, by cultural societies.

Now that Tommy was gone, an era seemed to have passed with him. I wondered if any of the men at the top of the B.B.C. in London knew anything about Tommy's work, and how much he had enriched broadcasting. In many ways he was like Priestley, vigorous in his independence and bigger than the B.B.C.

The day seemed to have been shattered by the news. "I'll make a cup of tea," said Mabel, "while you find out about the funeral."

I put in a call to the B.B.C., Manchester, and, as I waited, I took down Tommy's *Lancashire Pride,* a slim book with a grey cover. Published towards the end of the war, it contained a modest blurb on the jacket saying that Tommy's stories were popular with American soldiers stationed in the North.

Now, the Americans were back; or at least their younger brothers were. Times had changed; so had the faces. It didn't seem to matter very much why the Americans were in Warrington again so much as that they should like Tommy's work as their predecessors had done.

I looked at the inscription: "To my old pal Wilfred Pickles from T. Thompson." Then I found the story that sums up Tommy's style and outlook, my favourite among his writings. I sat down, started to read "Patience."

"Jim Dagnell leaned on the garden fence and spat on the good brown earth beneath. 'What's that tha'art sowin'?'

" 'Parsley,' said Sam.

" 'Parsley!' said Jim.

" 'Aye,' said Sam, 'parsley.'

"Jim turned this over in his mind before saying anything more. Then he said: 'So tha'rt tryin' parsley?'

" 'Aye,' admitted Sam, 'Ah'm tryin' parsley.'

" 'Ah've tried parsley misel',' said Jim. 'It con be very tryin' con parsley.'

" 'Ah know,' said Sam.

" 'It's all reet as long as tha knows,' said Jim. 'There's no harm in warnin' thee. Tha wants patience wi' parsley.'

" 'Tha wants patience wi' owt,' said Sam.

" 'But more so wi' parsley,' said Jim, 'nor owt.' "

Tommy's spirit sparkled in every line. This story and the rest were as fine a memorial to a life's work as any man could wish to have. I wondered whether to mention this in my letter of condolence to his family. Then I thought that perhaps it might be better just to say how sorry Mabel and I were. Sending sympathy to the bereaved is one of the hardest things one is called on to do.

As I drafted the few lines to the family, I recalled that, for the first time in the fifteen years I had worked with him, Tommy had brought them down to the studio to see his last programme being produced. He had with him his wife, son and daughter-in-law, and ten-year-old Jean, his grandchild. Tommy dedicated one of his books to her, and, in a line, told how life went on even in the midst of war: "To Jean," he wrote, "who brought a ray of sunshine into a blacked out world."

Tommy's funeral, said the B.B.C., Manchester, was to be on Monday. So Mabel and I started making arrangements to be there.

◻◻

CHAPTER SIX

Saturday

THE WARM SPRING SUNSHINE THAT HAD BECKONED US INTO Regent's Park had also brought out hundreds of holiday-makers and five-day-weekers. Peace comes suddenly in this lovely part of London: one minute you are darting a precarious path through four lines of accelerator-happy drivers and hooting horns, and the next you are clear of the fumes, the exhausts and the interminable hurry of the streets.

We watched the family groups laughing and romping on the springy turf; men throwing balls for energetic dogs, and children scampering round. Here and there were isolated figures, sitting serenely on the freshly painted benches or lying full-length on the ground.

One man was sprawled out with his head resting in his clasped hands and his feet up on a bulky knapsack. His battered trilby covered most of his face, and only a stubble of beard and the most contented smile I have seen peered out.

Through the horizon of trees I noticed the Georgian terraces, so lasting and incredibly attractive. They made a perfect frieze for this picture of peace. Beyond, and what seemed to be an age and a lifetime away, was a world of reality troubled with war talk, rearmament and impositions on the very freedom that the bearded, horizontal man stood for. Yet the spirit of the scene—happy children, carefree faces, even the prams that were everywhere—reassured me that mankind is greater than its own creations, including the atom and hydrogen bombs.

As we left the park, a coach was unloading its trippers outside Madame Tussaud's near Baker Street. Without quite realizing what we were doing, we had joined them, and, once inside the cold, echoing hall, we made for the imitation

B.B.C. studio to see how my effigy was going on. I remembered how disappointed I was when I first saw it, and wondered if it might seem more like me this time.

When we reached that corner of the waxworks where the broadcasters are kept, we could not get near the exhibits for a group of goodhumoured Tynesiders who were bantering a silent Richard Dimbleby for his plumpness. Mabel and I stood in the shadowy background, listening with delight to a mixture of Geordie outspokenness, both about the modelling and the modelled; some original radio criticism that would have put Fleet Street's practitioners to shame, and a display of sheer buffoonery by one of the party in an open-necked sports shirt who had an imaginary conversation with Jimmy Edwards.

Then came an interlude that was at once satisfying and terrifying. From the depths of this group of folk a tiny voice piped up: "Does Wilfred Pickles *really* look like that?"

I was bursting to say: "Well, not exactly . . ." when an authoritative grown-up announced in a tone that implied he had been in *Have a Go!* at least a dozen times: "Ay, it's a good 'un of him!"

"But that isn't his jacket, not *really*," persisted the curious child.

"No," came an assuring reply from the knowing one, "there are thousands o' jackets just like it."

Mabel nudged me as I edged forward. "Say nowt," she joked. How I wanted to tell this youngster the right answers! I was desperately longing to make it clear that not only was the sports jacket mine, but I had paid nine guineas for it in Piccadilly, Manchester, and I had liked it better than any sports jacket I had ever worn.

I looked at the waxwork figures around me in this "studio" that was even more temporary than anything at the B.B.C. and thought of the well-known people who had once held their places there. They had gone the way of all wax. I remembered the words of that young man of Tussaud's as he stood over me while my hands and forearms were shaved so that the modellers could take a plaster-cast without hurting me: "We've melted down a Hollywood actor, a cricketer and a jockey to make you!" he said, without a flicker of emotion. "Not a bad mixture, eh?"

I shuddered to think that one day I would be similarly liquidated maybe for an "atomic comic." "Who's Who" is spattered with people who regard it as a hallmark of fame to be in Tussaud's. But I wonder how many of those who have been modelled have experienced not only the needs of vanity but the most sobering reminder of the transience of celebrity-hood.

As I watched the carefree Tynesiders I wondered if they knew the value of their own simple lives, uncomplicated by the morbid fear of being "taken out," stripped of their clothing, having their eyes gouged out and then being subjected to the final cruelty of melting down.

At least they were not beset by the humiliating prospect of having their eyes put in a drawer for use in some unknown successor who might well be a murderer. If only my effigy's eyes could speak they might well say to Richard Dimbleby's: "Last time I saw you, you were Carpentier and I was one of the Tolpuddle Martyrs!"

By now, some of the onlookers were impatient with broadcasters and one woman protested: "Come on, Alec! We 'aven't all day! An' I want to see the Chamber of Horrors!"

"Crippen," I said, "can still pack 'em in!"

It occurred to me that whatever the artist might do in films, on the stage or over the air, will never give him the permanent appeal of the man who plunges his next-door neighbour into an acid-bath.

Mabel and I walked home the long way round, through the park and out by the Zoo, where the road was deep in parked cars and crowds were arriving with their picnic food under their arms and their faith in the summery weather reflected in the macs they carried. They looked contented: they were enjoying life; they probably had their own anxieties in the pursuit of health, happiness and the answer to life itself. But not for them the quicksands of demagogy, the waxen frailties of fame. In this moment of philosophizing I envied them their happy anonymity and thought of Milton's lines:

88

"Fame is the spur that the clear spirit doth raise
(That last infirmity of noble mind)
To scorn delights, and live laborious days,
But the fair guerdon when we hope to find,
And seek to burst out into sudden blaze,
Comes the blind Fury with the abhorred shears,
And slits the thin-spun life."

I recalled the day, not very long ago, when the Savage Club Year Book arrived, and I opened it where I expected to find my own name among the list of members. I scanned down the catalogue, turned over two pages, without coming across it. My name was not included! Then I noticed I had been looking at the obituaries.

As we approached the flat and I realized that Mabel would have to start cooking, I said: "Let's have a snack lunch today. After all, we're supposed to be on holiday." So we went on walking, right into Marylebone High Street, that lively, jolly shopping centre that always reminds me of Saturday morning. It is so varied and cosmopolitan that it could only be in London, yet it takes me back to Halifax, to the bustle of Saturday when everybody comes to life and to market. As a building apprentice and an outfitter's assistant in Halifax, I used to thrill to the crowds who made the sixth day the high-spot of the week. The town put on its best appearance and had all the atmosphere of a big city, with its packed shops, people coming in from smaller towns and nearby villages to shop, to watch a football match and to go to the pictures at night.

Saturday morning was worth looking forward to; somehow it used to make me feel quite important. On this glorious Saturday morning in 1951, Marylebone High Street took me back three decades. The shops were busier than those in Halifax; they appealed to a greater range of tastes, including the most eccentric; and the newsagents' stands were more worldly. We passed a dignified little shop where once Mabel and I, newcomers to London at the time, had called to buy some drinking glasses. We had asked for half a dozen, and the man behind the counter, who wore a blue tie and a tolerant expression, produced six single ones, none of which matched.

"They're rather nice, but we were looking for . . ." Mabel began.

I sensed we were in the wrong shop. "How much are these?" I asked.

The shopkeeper, standing amid the work of craftsmen throughout the ages, pursed his lips, regarded us with the timeless expression of the true connoisseur, and told us they were between six and seven guineas each. His shop, quiet as a cathedral, was certainly not the place for our mundane, rather Philistine, needs.

We walked on, absorbing the heady atmosphere of Marylebone High Street, enjoying its life and pace and its amusing contrasts: we noted the rare books next to the butchers' hooks; the antiques and golden chandeliers from princes' ballrooms hobnobbing with United Dairies and greengrocers' shops.

And all the time we kept one eye open for familiar faces in this vast, parochial metropolis. How often during our Saturday morning shopping expeditions down the High Street have we seen the tall, spare figure of Baliol Holloway, a sprightly six-footer in his late sixties, striding along with the same commanding air as in the days when he bestrode the Shakespearian stages. And how often have we exchanged a greeting with Phyllis Neilson-Terry, as she bought her weekend vegetables!

Mabel knows more of these "locals" than I do. She nodded and smiled and called "Good morning" to several people, and each time I asked, "Who was that?" Twice she replied, "Nobody you know," which made me all the more anxious to hear more about them.

Back in Halifax or Southport it might have been the plumber or the local music teacher or even a town councillor; in Marylebone High Street it is more often than not an actor, a student at the Royal Academy of Dramatic Art, a B.B.C. producer or a voice on the radio. Our own near-neighbours include Derek Oldham, Norman Shelley, Norman Wooland, Alastair Sim, Bruce Belfrage and Godfrey Tearle, as well as Eric Fawcett, the television producer, and Harry Alan Towers, the one-man competitor of the British Broadcasting Corporation.

Nothing was more certain than that we should come across at least one of our radio neighbours, and sure enough, outside the baker's shop where Mabel had bought a small loaf, we met Ted Kavanagh. Plump, colourful, untidy Ted is the most comfortable man I have even known. He is so easy-going that he has the effect of slowing me down, of settling me into a gentle tempo that is as good as a rest.

We strolled along, talking about *Itma*, which Ted scripted, telling stories about Tommy Handley and Jack Train, and exchanging views about Ted's show, *The Great Gilhooley*, which had not had too happy a time.

Ted looked at us, upwards through his bushy eyebrows, and said: "The critics killed it before it started. We couldn't live up to the reputation they built for it!" He shrugged his shoulders and added: "But it wasn't such a bad idea, you know!"

Every time we meet, Ted and I swop stories, and he genuinely enjoys a good tale. He rarely musters so much as the glimmer of a smile, but his sense of humour is sharp. I told him about the little boy from a working-class district where, when an increase is expected in the family, the first person to be called in is grandmother. He went to school one morning, approached the teacher and said: "Please, miss, we've got a new baby at our house!"

The young teacher nodded and replied: "That's nice. You know, I'd like a little baby, too!"

The boy looked concerned and knowledgeable. "Well, miss," he said, "all you have to do is to have a bath, put a clean nightie on and send for my granny!"

This led Ted and me into that interminable argument of ours, which neither of us believes has any point anyway, about the respective merits of the created humour of the gag-writers and the spontaneous quips of ordinary folk. From time to time Ted clears out of London and mixes with the fishermen, the weavers, the engineers and the housewives in provincial markets up and down the country, just to keep in touch with life and to feed his fertile imagination.

He knows the value of getting among the ordinary people and away from the entertainment machines of the West End, yet he usually challenges me by implying that humour comes from writers and not reality. He was delighted by the story I told him about Harriet Washington, a real Lancashire lass who came into one of my television shows. She hails from Shaw, a bleak little mill town that is definitely proud of its independence from Oldham.

Harriet, fat, jolly, came up to the camera in the grand manner, obviously one of those people who needs no bolstering up. She was so buoyant and cheerful that I asked her: "Is there anything you're afraid of, Harriet?"

"Oh, yes," she answered. "The atom bomb!" She winked confidingly and went on: "I'm afraid of putting any money in t'bank because of yon atom bomb!"

Then came an answer which, as I told Ted Kavanagh, the professional gag-writers would love to have invented. I asked Harriet what she liked doing more than anything else, and back it came, pat: "I love reading. I'm reading *Scott of the Antarctic* now. Oh, an' I'm that tired going over t'glaciers wi' 'em! I'm proper worn out!"

We asked Ted to come back to the flat for a drink, and on the way he mentioned that an idea he had developed two years earlier and which he had outlined to me in a Leeds hotel when I was playing in pantomime there, was now so clear that he would start writing it quite soon.

"You mean to say you've been thinking about it all this time? I thought you'd forgotten all about it," said Mabel.

Ted laughed. "Script-writers never stop thinking about gags and shows," he said.

"You're like us," Mabel said. "No holidays—not real ones, anyway."

"Next year . . ." I said.

"I know," she laughed. "Next year we'll really get away from it all."

But, holiday or no holiday, I was eager to hear more about Ted's programme-in-the-making. I was impressed by his tenacity in sticking to this idea which had appealed to me in its early stages, and I wondered if the radio critics, some of whom could be so scathing and bitter, realized that a slight hitch lasting seconds might shatter a brain-child that had been two years coming.

I knew how fair, understanding, tolerant and conscientious some critics could be, but how menacing were the others, not so much in their rôle as listeners' watchdogs, but as sensationmongers out for a scare headline! The thought brought back those memorable words Tommy Thompson had used: "Critics! Ah've shot 'em! Tha wants to use th' same approach to art an' music as tha does to good ale. Tha wants to get fuddled on 'em. Tha doesn't want to analyse 'em. Tha doesn't test a pint o' good ale wi' litmus paper. Sup it while it's fizzing. Tha can allus tell a critic. Just one long streak o' misery."

For an hour and more Ted outlined his idea. It sounded promising. It seemed the sort of material which, with luck and the right producer, might well become a winner. Even the synopsis Ted gave us was sprinkled with gags, a quality that made both *Itma* and *Take It From Here* great broadcasting shows; and I thought of an incident at the B.B.C. in Manchester years back when I saw Frank Randle, that fruity, gap-toothed northern comedian, turn down a script flat. He glanced through it, shrugged and exclaimed: "But— there's no gags!"

It was dramatic, and it was the end of a programme. Not for years did I learn the full significance of Frank's reaction.

Tommy Handley, Ted's partner for so many years, always had a lesson for the entertainer. He never stopped thinking in terms of gags; his scripts were packed with them, some from Ted Kavanagh, some from Francis Worsley, the producer of *Itma*, but many also from his own high-spirited conversation. Once, during the war and at the height of the bitter campaign in the Far East, he began to sing over the air a song that was popular in Britain at the time:

> "A-tisket, a-tasket,
> A little yellow basket!"

But he changed it to:

"A-tisket, a-tasket,
A little Japanee!"

There was also that well-remembered incident at
Bangor, where the B.B.C. Variety Department had been
evacuated in the dangerous years, when Tommy spotted one
of the members of the staff riding a bicycle through the town.
Attached to the handlebars was a basket full of scripts.
Tommy whooped: "It's the first time I've seen two baskets
on one bicycle!"

When Tommy died so suddenly and saddened a nation,
I was telephoned by a number of newspapers, asking me for
a tribute. I could only say: "We have lost the greatest of all
radio personalities and a wonderful man."

Tommy Handley was always so full of life, so uplifting,
and had such a vivid sense of humour that even the killjoys
and cynics must have tuned in to his broadcasts. He saw
comical caricatures in everyday things and people: Frisby
Dyke, the Liverpudlian who used to have Britain doubled
up with laughter, was the name of a shop I used to see often
on Merseyside, while it was a chance remark by Molly Weir
which Tommy captured and helped to make into one of the
catchphrases of *Itma*.

He was having a joke at Molly's expense during a break
in rehearsal when she exclaimed: "Och, man, you're da'aft!"

Tommy's eyes flashed. He pointed ecstatically at Molly.
"We're going to use that," he enthused.

One day in Manchester I was announcing Tommy on
the air and he told me of one of his experiences during the
blackout. He was playing Oldham at the time, and after the
first night, left the theatre to find the streets black and
deserted. He wandered on, but could not find his hotel. He
came on a man, just in front of him, carrying a torch. Tommy
followed.

Presently he spotted a landmark that gave him his bear-
ings, and he stepped into a shop doorway to light his pipe.
As he did so, two girls went by; there was a giggle, and one

of them called: "Look at that chap with his torch on all t'time!"

The stranger, hearing the remark, stopped in his tracks. "I suppose you live 'ere?" he asked solemnly.

"Yes, we do," they chorused.

"I reckon you'll know every stick and stone of this 'ere road?"

"I suppose we might."

"Ay," came the rejoinder. "Well, I'm a stranger—and to me it's like walking on a b—— precipice!"

That was the humour Tommy loved. It was the sort of ordinary material that he wove into sparkling fantasy, into that radio cartoon that was both real and unreal, the product of both individual genius and practical teamwork. And what a team that *Itma* trio was! Now here was Ted, the remaining member, still searching for the stories, experiences, characters and phrases that would make people laugh.

We decided to try to build up Ted's programme idea quietly, and agreed that the best way was to allow it to creep up on the listeners and the critics—from the cool shade of the North Region. *Have a Go!* had grown from small beginnings. There seemed no reason why another show could not do the same.

We chatted on about broadcasting. I said how often I despaired of the personal basis of B.B.C. work and resented the power of men who were qualified letter-writers, and apparently gifted in no other way, to play ducks and drakes with others' careers.

One evening when the head of one of the B.B.C. services came to our flat for tea, I told him: "I realize that if for some reason *Have a Go!* could not be broadcast and the announcer put on instead six gramophone records of Bing Crosby and Judy Garland, nobody would mind very much. I know the B.B.C. has given me regular work, for which I am grateful. You have helped to establish my name. But I don't understand you. I don't know what's going on at the back of your minds."

Mabel, Ted and I talked on about the future of radio work in Britain. We speculated about the B.B.C. monopoly and the Beveridge Report. We also got on to the subject of teamwork, and the advantages of being left alone to do a job in one's own way.

Ted was as full of enthusiasm for the new show he had in mind as a schoolboy usually is with a new pair of football boots that still have to be tried and tested. As he left, we shook hands and then waved him off; and, as he went down the stairs, he turned and called, "You never know."

Talking of the B.B.C. brought back memories of Tommy Thompson. What a spirit! What a writer! The B.B.C. needs as many Tommy Thompsons as it can find.

It was tragic that, in the morning, we should be travelling north in order to be at Tommy's funeral.

"This is one time," I said to Mabel as we walked back from the garage after putting the car away, "when I'm really not looking forward to going north."

"I know how you feel," came the reply. "But we must be there."

We went to bed early that night so that we would be fresh for the journey.

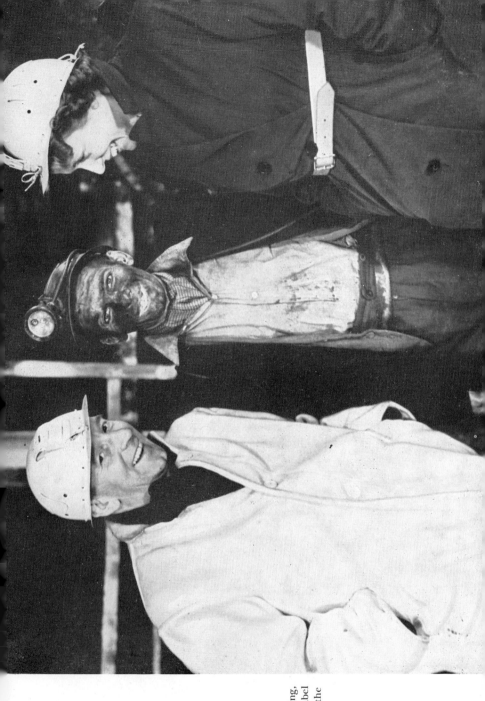

Ready for anything, Wilfred and Mabel get "shown the works."

Above: "Anything you can blow, I can blow harder!"

Below: Wilfred as the Charity Auctioneer, aboard the *Queen Mary*.

CHAPTER SEVEN

Sunday

LONDON, LYING IN, HAD HARDLY BEGUN TO STIR ITSELF AS we drove out through Finchley and the more obscure suburbs. The milkmen and the newsboys were still about, and outside one of the underground stations a man with all the Sunday papers was serving some half-dozen middle-aged customers.

Even on the best of days, the road to Manchester never inspires joy in the traveller; for it has neither the wide, open spaciousness of the American highways, which make me want to whistle, nor the narrow, mysterious corners to be found in Cornwall and parts of Lancashire and Yorkshire.

It offers a dull procession of indifferent towns and villages and a countryside that looks neither positively robust nor negatively unproductive. And on a grey, murky day such as this, the journey is only bearable because of the destination at the end of it.

There was precious little traffic about, though every mile or two we came upon a heavily laden lorry crawling sullenly north to Liverpool or south to London.

But as we approached the Midlands, through Fenny Stratford and Stony Stratford, those unlively villages where every day seems to be half-closing day, and nobody so much as breaks into a trot or a shout, we noticed streams of shining saloon cars moving in the opposite direction, to some southern docks for export.

"So that's where all the new cars are going," remarked Mabel.

I pointed to the beef sandwiches in her lap. "We've got to eat," I said.

On our road journeys to Manchester we always picnic.

My wife fills a flask, makes half a dozen sandwiches and packs two pieces of cake. It is a habit dictated by experience; for we have often gone miles along Watling Street trying to get a meal, and twice within a week were served with lunches that were not properly cooked.

There was also the time when we tried to get some meat. Mabel had brought our ration cards and we stopped at a butcher's shop in the main street of one of these in-between places which are as isolated as Eskimo camps. He had no meat at all. He put his hands on his hips, said nothing and pointed at the empty hooks with a skewer.

Perhaps it was that incident that left us with the unalterable conviction that there is no food to be had between London and Manchester, and that A5 is the road to hunger and despair unless you take a flask and a snack and a good travelling companion.

Fortunately we never stop talking once we get going; and the miles slide away on a helter-skelter of conversation that has touched just about every subject there is by the time we approach Lichfield.

With places like Atherstone, Tamworth and Weedon behind, the worst of the trip is over. Though they are built round one of the busiest and most important roads in Britain they are like communities of the lost; they seem remote, but not in the enchanted way like Looe and Enniskillen, Keswick, and Richmond in Yorkshire.

The whole character of these places is one of inferiority. Perhaps they are frustrated and forced within themselves because so many travellers pass through without taking the trouble to stop and take notice of them. I invariably try to get an idea of what is going on in these places by keeping an eye open for posters advertising shows, films, concerts, lectures, personal appearances and other community entertainment; but I am usually more baffled and disturbed than ever by the time we have left their narrow shopping streets behind and are back on the open road.

Often Mabel has remarked: "What they need is a bit of fun!" I have recognized this as a challenge to take *Have a Go!* among them; but somehow I am not at all sure that they would make up the happy, responsive audience to be found anywhere else in these islands. Yet these people are no doubt as proud of the Stratfords, of Weedon, Atherstone and the rest as I am of Yorkshire and as the Londoner is of being born within earshot of Big Ben.

They will, I am sure, have a go at me for writing so critically of their home towns. I remember a few years ago, at a London house party, several guests were making scathing comments about the name and architectural appearance of Sowerby Bridge, a smoky little township of black stone factories and old terrace houses in the Calder Valley. Suddenly, the unanimity was shattered by a young man who piped up and said calmly: "Don't forget that Sowerby Bridge spells H-O-M-E to some of us!"

This local pride is stronger by far than many people, including politicians, newspapermen and entertainers, are inclined to give it credit for. I have got used to meeting, on my travels up and down Britain, the emigrants within our borders; the folk who have moved from Glasgow to Glamorgan and love to recall Sauchiehall Street and the Hampden roar; the couples from Bolton and Bradford who, in their retirement, have gone to live in Bournemouth and still thrill to the memory of the mills and the black sky that heralds not a storm at sea but a thriving industry and full employment.

There are the people who cut themselves away from familiar faces and surroundings to find warmth, fresher air or money and influence. Some succeed in securing greater comfort or in "getting to the top," but they can never quite cut themselves adrift from their native towns or villages. They come to me wherever I go with *Have a Go!*

They shake hands, old and young alike, unemotional business men and sentimental spinsters, and say with almost spaniel-like affection: "Halifax, Wilfred! Halifax!" It is sometimes embarrassing, especially if I have only recently been back in the dark valley of my birth; for I am not always deeply touched by the memory of it all. At such times I pass it over with a gag. "It's all right," I say, "but you've got away, I notice."

99

As for the districts that border Watling Street, they must surely engender similar loyalties. And perhaps, after all, they are not so dull; for, on the few occasions when we travel to Manchester by train, I have noticed that they look different from the back. Probably the wireless aerials that abound give me a different picture. At least, they suggest that Atherstone. Weedon and Tamworth are not such isolated outposts as their main streets imply: they are populated by people who listen to, and look at, the world they live in. And, as B.B.C. listeners, they will be represented in the Listener Research findings. It is a sobering thought that the folk of these A5 communities can tell the B.B.C. that they have heard enough of me and have me cast out to the West End theatre or that fantastic film world of which they are healthily clear.

As we pulled into lovely Lichfield, with its awesome cathedral testifying to the finest qualities of good taste and public service in mankind, we stopped by the kerbside and lingered. Here, quite suddenly, was a part of England that lived up to the poets' visions of our country; friendly, peaceful, its public buildings and private houses blending in serene architectural harmony.

"If I were a visitor to England," said Mabel, "this would make my stay." Across the threshold of the afternoon came the Sunday sounds of church bells, gracious "Good mornings" exchanged across a quietened street, and the intruding hoot of a car horn. Here and there there were little groups of boys and girls, tidily on their way to Sunday school. Coming upon such a scene, after the miles of colourless anonymity, was like diving for a pebble and coming across a pearl-oyster.

I followed with my eyes the line of the delicate steeples of Lichfield Cathedral and recalled those words of Congreve's:

"How reverend is the face of this tall pile,
Whose ancient pillars rear their marble heads
To bear aloft its arched and ponderous roof,
By its own weight made steadfast and immovable,
Looking tranquillity!"

100

Sunday

When I looked down again there was another parked car on the opposite side of the road, a sprawling surge of grey-white streamlining with a plump, bronzed man in a wide-brimmed hat and rimless spectacles at the wheel.

"Americans!" I said.

"They haven't got anything like that in li'l ole New York," Mabel shot back.

"Go and tell them that," I said. "I'll dare you!"

"I'll mind the car while you go," Mabel laughed.

I burst out laughing.

"Remember San Francisco?"

During our holiday in the U.S.A. we had been introduced to a friendly business man in San Francisco who was intensely proud of his city. He took us round in his Cadillac, droning on all the time about the world's biggest, highest, greatest, heaviest, deepest, fastest and most lovely.

I began to nod off, and I could see Mabel had been hypnotized into a similar state by the sun and the sound of the man's monotone. She kept half-closing her eyes, and our guide's superlatives were probably drifting miles away from her.

"And this," he went on, explaining the origins and development of a big store that rose like a precipice to our left, "is a miracle of business."

There was more, and more still, about San Francisco. Suddenly, in an effort to justify the expenditure of so much enthusiasm on us, Mabel murmured: "And what is the population?"

"Seven hundred thousand," came the reply.

"Including the Chinese?" came Mabel's sleepy rejoinder.

It stumped our guide for the first time. It stirred me into life. Nowadays, when Mabel is trying to keep conversation going with friends and visitors, I often whisper to her: "Including the Chinese?"

I started the car up, just as the Americans were getting out of theirs, and as we picked up speed I caught a last glimpse of the cathedral and remembered Wordsworth's lines:

"They dreamt not of a perishable home
Who thus could build."

Lichfield, neat and sharp as a new pin, lived up to all
that was best in English social life, even on such a grey day
when the clouds were frowning. Mabel recalled the time we
had stopped for a cup of tea at a roadside café in the town
some months earlier and the jolly little proprietor had
proudly told us he had lived there for twenty years.

He stroked his chin and winked. "The only people
who have never made money here are the bookies," he said.

"How's that?" I asked, sensing a good story for *Have
a Go!*

A grin split his plump face. "They know how to pick
'em here!"

I wondered for a moment whether it was because the
good churchfolk of Lichfield kept clear of the horses or
whether they got such good tips that they beat the book-
makers on the course. Certainly, there was a striking
common factor about cathedral cities: that where spires
were predominant so also were people's little weaknesses.
In one cathedral city, it was fairly generally accepted that
the stranger could approach a policeman on point duty and
ask: "Where can I put a bet on?"

Between his signals to traffic, he would say: "Down
there, turn left. The pub's closed but there's a little side
door. You'll be all right!"

Personally, I think off-course betting is a mug's game,
and I would prefer to stake a couple of shillings on flies
crawling up a window than on racehorses that I have no
chance of seeing. People trying to be friendly and helpful
give me tips every day, but the only time I take any notice
of them is just before the Grand National and the Derby,
when I have half a crown on and Mabel a shilling. Once,
when I met the great Steve Donoghue, he gave me three
tips for the following day, none of which came anywhere
near.

But I had the opposite experience with Gordon
Richards. I was talking to him the day before he was due to

ride in the Lincoln. "I'll win tomorrow, you know," he said confidently. I passed on the tip to several friends, who all backed Gordon's horse, Dramatic. I knew better than to put money on a horse on the strength of a jockey's confidence. I had completely forgotten Dramatic on the day of the race and bought an evening paper for the news rather than the racing. As the newspaper seller fumbled for the change he said: "Well, Gordon's pulled it orf again, guvnor!"

"Did you hear that?" asked Mabel. "What did it win at?"

"Eight to one," came the answer.

For weeks after that I had to live down rumours among B.B.C. people who call at our flat that Mabel and I had won hundreds on Dramatic. One actor winked and said: "Keeping it dark again, eh?"

The only time I have won money on a horse was shortly after a *Have a Go!* programme in which I interviewed a middle-aged lady whose hobby, she said, was backing horses.

"Oh," I replied, "and what's going to win the big race tomorrow?"

She shook her head solemnly, and in her eyes was all knowledge. "I can't tell all these people!"

"Well, whisper, luv!"

She did. Confidingly, she said: "Master Vote." I framed the words back at her. She nodded. The horse won at sixteen to one.

My thoughts of horse-racing and plump bookies with big houses, two cars and a gardener were interrupted by Mabel, who said: "Look at this horrible stuff pouring out!"

We were passing a nest of kilns on the roadside, for all the world like primitive ovens at some witches' camp, but in fact a part of our industrial machine. It was a tile-making plant. The chimneys over the kilns were short; and thick, brown-green fumes drifted across the road and into the car.

We coughed our way through it, and looked down from the hill we were climbing to the Five Towns, huddled under an umbrella of smoke. It seemed hard to believe that so much beautifully designed china, delicate and artistic enough for the most fastidious tastes all over the world, could come out of such a sooty, fearful cauldron. I felt I would like to lift the little houses right out of the smoke-pall into the sunlight of the surrounding hills, so that its people would get fresh air, instead of filth, into their lungs.

The odd-town-out of the Potteries, Newcastle-under-Lyme, was quiet, but lorries were trundling through in both directions. "Nice to get through without any traffic jams," I remarked. We are both accustomed to being held up temporarily in Newcastle, which on weekdays must be one of the most confused places in Britain, with its main street packed with commerce on the move. It is just south of this ill-shaped town that the main road from Manchester, Liverpool, Warrington and the other great producing centres of Lancashire branches into two—one to London and the south, the other to the Midlands.

I am always glad to get beyond Newcastle on the way up; for then our route takes us through the mellow lanes and tidy villages of Cheshire, with its tree-bordered roads and undisturbed gentleness. As we passed Little Moreton Hall, a finely beamed Tudor house now being cared for by the National Trust, some cyclists were turning towards it. Even in the drizzle of a dampening day, the sight of the place filled me with optimism and I felt thankful that the Trust had taken over what might have been prostituted by selfish speculators.

I thought of a part of the coast of Cornwall which had been similarly adopted in the public interest to be preserved for all times as a beauty spot instead of being allowed to deteriorate into building land; and of Ayot St. Lawrence, Shaw's home. Mabel and I had been promising ourselves a visit to the playwright's home for months, and one of the greatest regrets of my life is that I failed to take up an invitation from Shaw to visit him. Early in 1950 I was writing a series of articles for a national newspaper and Mabel suggested I ought to do one on the superstitions of well-known people and folk I had met while touring with *Have a Go!*

Sunday

I immediately thought of Bert Middleton, of Looe, a sturdy, broad-shouldered and broad-minded fellow with a voice that fills the microphone; for once he had told me of the superstitions and dreads of the local fishermen. I telephoned Bert, who recalled that they would never launch a new boat or go to sea for the first time on a Friday.

"No daffodils in the house for us, either," he went on. "We call 'em Lent Lilies. And you'll never find Cornish fishermen using Cornish granite to weight their lobster pots down."

I was so pleased with this answer that I started making a list of people I might telephone to ask them their superstitions. There was Hermione Gingold, Len Hutton, Gordon Richards and a stranger in the telephone book. I counted thirteen pages, found a phone number ending in thirteen with digits adding up to thirteen. The subscriber turned out to be a surprised housewife who admitted she was afraid of breaking mirrors, spilling salt, walking under ladders, and Friday the thirteenth.

As I was talking to her, and laughing at her answers— "It had never dawned on me that my phone number had so many thirteens in it," she exclaimed—Mabel had an idea.

When I put the telephone down, she said: "Why don't you ring George Bernard Shaw?"

"Shaw won't have any superstitions. He'd just laugh at me," I replied.

Mabel, who was writing a letter, looked up. "Don't be so sure. He's Irish—and he has an imagination."

I found Shaw's number, and as I held on while it rang out, I was tempted to call the whole thing off. I put a hand over the mouthpiece. "I feel daft about this," I said.

"He can only say 'No,' " she reassured me.

A woman's voice answered. I explained who I was and what I wanted.

"Just a minute," she said.

In a few seconds she was back. "Yes, Mr. Shaw will have a word with you. But speak very slowly—he is a very old man, you know."

I could picture the bearded genius shuffling along to-

105

wards the phone, his eyes glistening and his brain working on a short answer to such an intruder. Then came a hesitant Irish brogue: "Yes, young man, what is it you want?"

I explained briefly what I was doing.

"I would love to help you, young man. But you—you must give me a little time to think. I am an old man."

"Surely," I said.

Shaw's voice came back again: "You know, I am only talking to you now because my housekeeper is your biggest fan. I need time to think. You must come out and see me, will you?"

The invitation thrilled and surprised me. Mabel was over the moon. "We'll go next week," she said. "We must," I added.

But something cropped up to prevent us going the following week. In fact, we never got round to it at all; and a few months later the greatest playwright of our age was dead.

A dripping signpost pointing to Macclesfield brought me back into the present. Soon we would be back in Manchester, with the rain gurgling down its gutters like cocoa and the clouds crying their eyes out. The thought reminded me of the story of the Cockney sparrow that hopped into a goods van at Euston, pecking at corn on the floor. The door was suddenly slammed shut and the sparrow found itself at London Road Station, Manchester. It hopped out into the fog and drizzle, and spotted another bird.

"Wotcher, me ole cock sparrer?" called the Cockney.

The other bird twittered back: "I don't know thee! I've never met thee! Don't talk to me!"

"Blimey!" retorted the Cockney sparrow. "Can't one cock sparrer talk to another cock sparrer?"

The Manchester bird replied: "Ah'm tellin' thee! I don't know thee! I've never met thee! An' what's more, I'm not a cock sparrow." And rubbing the mud off his breast with a claw, said: "Look, I'm a robin!"

Through the drizzle and the mist, I noticed the road forking to the right which led into Derbyshire, that wonderland of limestone precipices and gaunt peaks, always one of my favourite districts. I muttered some of the Derbyshire village names that roll so smoothly off the tongue: "Millersdale, Dovedale, Baslow," and Mabel reminded me that I have slipped into the habit of unconsciously speaking these names whenever we get within striking distance of Derbyshire.

Then we were in our own village, Disley, with its views over thousands of acres of pastures, its mixture of big houses, "semis" and cottages. It was good to be alive on such a day with the rain splashing the windscreen and the tyres singing on the gleaming tarmac. This was the north—wet, grey, muggy; the north of contrasts, of family life, of friendly, animated folk who knew how to live and how to fight for existence; the north of Priestley and the *Manchester Guardian* and Gracie Fields, where social barriers were small ones and where morning suits and striped trousers were still regarded with suspicion.

Here was the village where we had only recently bought a house, a microcosm of the whole of this fabulous north of England, a half-way house between workaday Manchester and the poetry of the Derbyshire landscape.

"We'll be able to slip over and take the waters," I said.

"The waters?" Mabel queried.

"At Buxton," I said.

"Are they as good as the Harrogate waters?"

"Well, I once knew a chap who sampled the free supply at Harrogate and, spitting it out, said: 'No wonder they give it away for nowt!'"

As we drew into the drive, there with a welcome on the doorstep was Mabel's mother, wiping her hands on her apron. "I thought you were never coming!" she said. I looked at my watch. We were twenty minutes late. "Not bad in this weather," I said.

Inside the house, we found tea already laid—for five. Mabel's mother had visitors, an elderly couple who are too shy to have their names mentioned in a book.

They are the sort of characters who might have come to life in any of the great northern novels; typically Lancashire and full of wonder and suspicion about the world beyond their own county. Once I was describing them to friends in London and purposely avoided mentioning their name. "Call them Mr. and Mrs. Birtwistle," said Mabel. I did; and it seemed to fit. Mr. and Mrs. Birtwistle will do for this narrative, too.

As soon as we got in, Mrs. Birtwistle stuck her chin in and looked over her spectacles and exclaimed: "I don't know how you do it. I say I don't know how you do it!"

"Do what?" I began.

"Travel up and down like this. It'd put us out, wouldn't it, Albert. I say it'd put us out!"

Albert agreed, as he always agrees; for he is an affable, genial soul who says little and gives the impression of being thoughtful. He used to be a designer in calico printing, a job that affords plenty of opportunity for mental activity. Mrs. Birtwistle is uncontrollably sociable, out to practise good manners and consideration for others, and I had not been in the room more than a moment after having a wash than she looked across at her husband, sitting stiffly in my favourite armchair, and prompted: "Get up, Albert, and let 'im sit down—he'll be tired!"

She folded her hands in her vast lap and said in a much quieter tone: "I bet the sun was out down south!"

We tried to explain that the weather was no different in London, but Mrs. Birtwistle was away on one of her reminiscences. Like most of her talk, it was full of repetitions, prefaced by the words "I say."

"We once went for a holiday in the south, didn't we, Albert? I say we once had a holiday down south—at Mablethorpe!"

The table talk drifted from one neighbour of the Birtwistle's to another, with Mrs. Birtwistle getting in an occasional "Tut, tut" of refined horror as well as her customary exclamation: "I don't know what things are coming to, I really don't! I say I don't know what things are coming to!"

Dear old Mrs. Birtwistle. She puts whisky in her tea; she loves people, and she takes the whole social scene of births, marriages and deaths with that air of calm amazement and resigned curiosity that is the hallmark of the real Lancastrian. For a while she entertained us with a story about her next-door neighbours. "He's got a better job," she announced. "You know, he used to be a gatekeeper at t'football ground. Well, he's in t'directors' office now. Knows 'em all!

"After every game they 'ave a party and he cleans up after they've gone. It's a much better job an' they tell 'im everything. I say it's a lot better na being at t'turnstiles. He wor allus a bob or two short!"

Another neighbour, it transpired, had been having a bad time with rheumatism, and Mrs. Birtwistle's own grand-daughter had recently celebrated her fifth birthday with a party. "They gave 'er a surprise," said Mrs. Birtwistle. "They got all the kids together in a room and then put the lights out to bring in the cake with all its candles lit. Oh, an' you know what little Joan said? She said: 'Ooh, Mummy, it's a power cut!'"

Mabel's mother brought in our meat ration—two pieces of pork, done to a crackle. I wondered whether I would ever enjoy pork so much when I could have a whole leg and yards of crackle. Now, rationed and scarce, it was one of life's joy, like holidays, and the first day of spring, and good listening figures. We looked at our portions as if they were Koh-i-noor diamonds.

"You're here for Mr. Thompson's funeral, aren't you?" asked Mrs. Birtwistle. I nodded. It was strange to hear Tommy described as Mr. Thompson; I had never heard his formal name used before.

After tea, Mabel joined the others round the fire and I went browsing among my books, finding now and again with delight an edition I had forgotten I ever possessed and coming across lines of poetry that were in tune with my mood. I made notes on a scrap of paper to use these discoveries in one of my poetry programmes on the air. There was poetry to fit my own voice; the lilting lines of Burns that would be so well spoken by James McKechnie, and one particular poem by John Betjeman seemed to have been written for Arthur Marshall.

I recalled the party Mabel and I had given in our flat for the recording of one of these poetry readings in *The Pleasure's Mine* series. Outside, in Devonshire Street, was a B.B.C. van loaded with equipment, with wires trailing into the building. Our lounge was so hot—there were about forty people in it—that we opened one of the windows. Finally, after much fuss and banter, we started the recording.

Everything was going well until, during Peggy Ashcroft's reading, a raucous voice raised in drunken song floated in from the street. It was the very opposite of Peggy's delicate, poised delivery. I waved frantically towards one of the engineers. Somebody went to the window, peered outside and put a finger to his lips in a gesture that called for silence.

But the songster went on, oblivious of the stir he had caused or of the rude impact of his voice on Peggy's poetry.

I collected three or four books of poetry and stacked them in the window-ledge with the intention of taking them back to London. Outside, there was still a fine drizzle, and a light mist had settled down in the valley.

The green fields and leafy trees looked healthy enough, and I wondered idly why no cattle or sheep were grazing on the hillsides. I remembered those acres up on the harsh, exacting Pennines where once a foreign visitor stood in awe as a "local" pointed out the cattle spread out across the bleak moors.

"Doesn't seem much for them to eat up there," said the visitor.

The "local" wiped his mouth with the back of his hand. "P-raps not," he said. "But look what a grand view they've got!"

I had been among my books for about an hour when Mabel's mother called: "They're going now, Wilfred!" I ran downstairs to bid Mr. and Mrs. Birtwistle goodbye. Albert was already at the front door, his hat and walking-stick in one hand and a carrier bag in the other. His wife was still inside the vestibule, beckoning me in that confidential manner characteristic of so many northern folk.

"Just one thing I wanted to know," she confided. "Are these radio critics allowed in the B.B.C.?"

I assured her they knew everybody at the B.B.C. She shook her head in bewilderment. "London," she pronounced, "must be a very queer place. I say it must be a very queer place!"

And the look she gave me was even more eloquent than her words! It reminded me of the Lancashire lad who went to London for the first time in his life and was taken out into the West End for a meal by a friend.

"Where would you like to go?" he was asked.

"Not bothered," he replied.

Finally, they went into a famous Indian restaurant noted for its spicy and uncommon dishes. The waiter approached their table, bowed and presented the menu.

The Lancashire man looked down the list of courses, up at the waiter, across at his friend, then back at the menu and said: "I'll tell thee what it is, mate! I'll 'ave a salad and play for safety!"

Throughout the meal he said nothing. He watched the other diners, some in evening dress, and kept a close eye on the tips. As they were leaving he went to the cloakroom for his overcoat and again noticed the lavish gratuities.

The attendant handed him his coat, for which the Lancastrian gave him a two-shilling piece, and then started fumbling for change.

"Keep it!" came the Lancashire voice. "Keep it, lad! Buy thisel' a ruddy cotton mill!"

This was the humour of Lancashire.

A bus came along the road and drew up just beyond our gate. "Pickles Corner," came the conductor's call.

"What was that?" Mabel asked.

"Sounded like——" I began.

"It was," said Mabel's mother resignedly. "They know you're living here now. They've called it after you!"

We were back in the north all right. And there seemed little danger that we would ever be lost among these folk!

■□

CHAPTER EIGHT

Monday week

I WAS OUT IN THE GARDEN, TAKING IN THE ATMOSPHERE OF our new home and viewing it from all angles, when Mabel opened a ground-floor window and called: "Phone, Pickles, you're wanted!"

With our Kerry Blue pup at my heels spoiling for a game, I made towards the window, and answered from outside. The caller was the parson who would be taking the service at Tommy's funeral.

"I was wondering," he said, "if you would like to read the lesson."

"Delighted to," I replied. We talked for a few moments about Tommy's grand work, his personality and shining humour. The reading, I was told, would be the usual one which goes: "And God shall wipe away all tears from their eyes. . . ."

It was only when I had put the telephone down that I realized that my navy-blue suit, which would not have looked out of place among a group of people, was hardly right for the lesson reader in church.

I looked around for Mabel, called her, and heard an answering shout from the kitchen. "I'm reading the lesson this afternoon," I told her. "Do you know where my striped trousers, coat and vest are?" Mabel was leaning over a steaming sink loaded with dishes. She looked round and answered: "They're in the wardrobe in London."

"That's done it," I exclaimed.

"You'll have to get another, or borrow one!"

Five minutes later I was in the car and on the way to Manchester. Mabel had agreed to cancel arrangements we had made with a B.B.C. producer and a cotton mill director to entertain them during the morning; and I felt thankful that these diplomatic jobs had not fallen to me.

I remembered the time, years before, when I borrowed clothes from a well-known firm of theatrical costumiers in the city, and now I made for the same shop. The assistant directed me to a changing-room, and there I tried on the trousers.

"A bit drainpipy, aren't they?" I said, perturbed by the sight in the mirror in front of me. The man pursed his lips and shrugged. Then, like a magician holding a rabbit by the ears, he produced the jacket. It had short lapels and three buttons!

I looked again, rather reluctantly, in the mirror. "Crimes!" I muttered. "Mr. Pecksniff!" I was shocked and discouraged, but the look on the assistant's face made it plain that it was this or "nowt." Somewhere, perhaps, Tommy was looking down on me and having as great a laugh as he always got out of the embarrassing moments and quirks of character that turned up in everyday life.

The assistant coughed. I nodded. "All right," I said. "I'll have it!" All the way back in the car I was regretting having borrowed this Dickensian outfit, and I wondered what Mabel and her mother would think of it.

Mercifully, they said it wasn't bad. I knew Mabel thought otherwise, but I would never have risked asking her to be really frank about it. To make things worse, I had cut my chin while shaving and had had to put some sticking-plaster on the wound.

The funeral was planned for half-past two, and Mabel and I had been invited by Donald Stephenson, North Region Controller, and Bob Stead, Head of Programmes, to join them in the staff car. We arrived in Bury earlier than we had expected, so I said: "Let's slip in and have a drink!"

Suddenly, it occurred to me that this might seem out of place on such a sad occasion, but after a moment's thought I was reassured and certain that Tommy himself would have been the first person in the world to agree to the suggestion. I remembered the wonderful story he had once told me about the old man of Oldham who was ill in bed and felt that his end was near. He sent for his two pals, who entered the house quietly, took of their cloth caps and carefully wiped their feet on the mat.

As they entered the bedroom, he called: "Nah then, lads, ah've 'ad it!"

"Nay, nay," they chorused. "Come, come!"

"I'm tellin' yer," he persisted. "Ah'm done for!"

They hardly knew what to say. Then he went on: "There's one thing I'd like you to do. It's my last wish." They leaned closer to him.

He raised a tired arm and pointed towards the bottom of the bed. "In my waistcoat pocket theer tha'll find half a crown. I want you to promise me that when we go up to t'cemetery you'll stop by t'Rose and Crown, an' I want you to go in and 'ave a pint apiece—an' leave me out same as you've always done!"

Bury was cheerless and damp and in the shadow of Monday. A few housewives were out in the shopping centre, which has a Lilliputian air because of its low-level buildings; and here and there we saw the washing on the lines, not so conspicuous as it used to be, even in the immediate prewar years, but fluttering in the slight breeze like a scattered testimony to the settled permanence of home life in Lancashire. Here was another of those busy little mill towns that had helped to save Britain in peace and war, but of which the world heard little. Bury! Home of black puddings, those delicious butchers' concoctions that are served steaming hot. Its other claim to fame was won by one of its sons, Robert Peel; but it had also produced many distinguished men and women, including Richmal Crompton, the author of *Just William*.

Now we were on the outskirts of the town, I saw a signpost to Tottington, which I remembered boasts a fine concertina band. Once, Tommy showed me round the place and got the band to give us a show. They kept on playing tune after tune, long after Tommy and I had fully appreciated their talent, and Tommy whispered: "T'only way to stop 'em is to stun one of 'em!"

The north abounds with bands of all descriptions that

parade the streets on field days and at Whitsuntide treats and infirmary processions. Their music is not judged so much by its sound as by the distance covered while it is being played. At the band club meeting you might express a preference for "Blaze Away!" and find yourself squashed by: "That's no use! Acorn Street to t'War Memorial just teks t' 'March of the Gladiators' an' nowt else'll fit!"

The cemetery was chilly and damp as all graveyards seem to be on funeral days; and I was relieved, for the sake of Tommy's family, when it was all over. Tommy Thompson, I knew, was far from dead. His writings would endure; and I preferred Tommy as the man I knew, the writer who captured life with all the accuracy and none of the flatness of a photograph, the brilliant and modest man of letters who was as unaffected as he was sincere. And of all the delightful stories he had given us, the one I kept remembering, and will always regard as most typical of Tommy's love of ordinary folk, was *Pedigree Pup*.

It is a true story of a Lancashire couple who buy a pup and are assured it will not grow big, but soon see that it is likely to become a giant among dogs.

That is Tommy Thompson at his best. The story so tickled me that I included it in my solo act at the Opera House, Blackpool. George Black, the famous impresario, sat facing me on a chair that was placed the wrong way round, resting his elbows on its back, and said: "All right, Wilfred, let's go!"

This was the first rehearsal. I got into the story and soon saw that George Black was doubled up with laughter. He told me afterwards that *Pedigree Pup* had become one of his favourite stories. During subsequent rehearsals I heard stage hands and assistants calling it by another name: "The dog gag!"

The dog gag! It was like confusing dramatic poetry with the eroticism of shady verses written on walls. "If the variety theatre got hold of Shakespeare," I told George Black one day, "they would soon be talking about the Hamlet gag!"

This remark seemed to amuse him; for if anybody knew

show business and every trick and habit in the entertainment world, it was this husky, amiable and determined man who was always ready with good advice and encouragement. During one break in rehearsal we were talking about the American comedians who come over here and hold the stage on their own for an hour and more.

"I don't know how they do it," I said.

Black agreed. "Twelve minutes is enough for any artist to stay out there. There's no more lonely place in the world than the centre of the stage when you are a single act!"

Driving back to Manchester after the funeral, the B.B.C. men, Mabel and I got round to Tommy's contribution to radio and the importance of regional broadcasting. We were still on the same subject in Donald Stephenson's office in the unprepossessing B.B.C. building in Piccadilly.

I took the line that northern writers were not encouraged as they ought to be, that the north was teeming with tales and talent that were lost to the B.B.C. only because producers were not encouraged to go out after them.

"There's too much centralization in the B.B.C.," I said. "And that means that programmes get more and more divorced from real life and real people."

I remembered the early work of Geoffrey Bridson; some of the programmes by that talented features producer, Norman Swallow; and the work, mainly in print, of some newspaper men who clearly had the makings of brilliant radio feature writers.

Yet the B.B.C. had sent a London writer to develop a feature about Sheffield. To listeners who really knew the north, and especially the great steel city, it was clear that the author of the programme had never lived there, and knew precious little about it. I was approached to take the part of narrator; but I had another engagement on the evening the programme was broadcast.

I like feature work so much that I turned down the offer with a feeling of loss. But it was fortunate for me that I did, for the B.B.C. was lashed for broadcasting nonsense about mothers having to bath their children in sooty water. If I had been narrator I would have taken a share of the blame for such an irresponsible exaggeration. I may have objected to it during rehearsals, but there is nothing to say that any suggestion of mine would have been upheld.

The North Region bosses listened patiently as I developed my argument. I had said it all before to successive controllers and heads of programmes, but where there were willing ears there was always hope!

I explained that there were half a dozen journalists who could handle feature programmes efficiently and well, and who were capable of presenting a frank portrait of places, people and problems. Mayors and aldermen were notoriously touchy about the truth; but in some instances their complaints were merited. Liverpool is more than Lime Street in the early hours; it is not populated only or mainly by prostitutes, confidence men, spivs and dangerous aliens, and it has districts that are just as important as dockland and Aintree and the acres of football pools offices.

What I did not mention was that in *Have a Go!* we have always been careful to use a representative cross-section of the population and its interests.

We have taken the programme to every B.B.C. region, given attention to urban and rural districts, cities, towns and villages, centres and suburbs, pubs, clubs and industries. "You can't go wrong," I emphasized, "with real people and real life."

Of course, nobody can please all the people all the time and the B.B.C. often falls back on this truth as a facile explanation for its failures.

I have met many honest people who frankly said they could not bear *Have a Go!* Probably the best example of this minority viewpoint occurred when Mabel and I were on holiday in Switzerland. We were staying at a cosy little hotel in Wengen, a fairyland village where sleighbells can be heard and where our hotelier had a natural bar cut out of a snowdrift. Holes big enough to hold the bottles were drilled into the packed snow to make a sort of refrigerated wine cellar right out in the open!

We had been there two or three days before our host admitted that he listened to *Have a Go!* He had not wanted to mention it, he explained, because he thought we might want to escape from everything and hear nothing about the B.B.C. and even less from its listeners.

"We always like to hear about our programmes," I said.

The little man, warm of manner and with a gay charm that blended well with the happy-go-lucky atmosphere of his hotel in the hills, needed no further invitation.

He regaled us with tit-bits he recalled from some of our programmes, and finally asked me if I would do *Have a Go!* for him and the villagers—"and, of course, the English tourists"—in the hotel ballroom.

"All right," I said. "The night before we go!"

The following morning we were strolling through the village—cautiously because I had gone full-length soon after our arrival on the icy roads—when Mabel suddenly noticed that on nearly every tree was a notice with the words "Have a Go!" in large letters.

We went up close to one of these posters. "Wilfred Pickles will present his famous B.B.C. programme," it announced. In front of us, also reading it, was an elderly lady and a girl of about eighteen who was wearing slacks, sun-glasses, a roll-collar sweater and ski-ing boots.

"Oh, Auntie!" the girl exclaimed. "It's that dreadful programme where that frightful man wanted tea with senna pods!"

I nearly burst out laughing at the contrast between this girl with the chromium-plated accent and Ben Ainsworth, the rugged seventy-three year old Blackburn man, who had come out with this, the finest gem among the answers from ordinary folks given to my questions over the years.

"Suppose," I chuckled, as we went along, "suppose they're all like that lass?"

"Don't worry," came the reply. "They won't be!"

On the contrary, I found one of the most accommodating audiences I have ever known. There were scores of people from Britain, including many who seemed to have stepped right out of the pages of the *Tatler,* and I was doubtful until the very last moment about the kind of reception they would give to the show.

But everything went off with such good fun that our host delightedly shook hands with us and said: "Come, we must have breakfast!"

"Breakfast!"

He made a gesture with his thumb and middle finger. "You will enjoy it, yes."

That was how Mabel and I came to be out in the ice-sharp Swiss night on our way to a two-o'clock-in-the-morning meal of bacon and eggs. Surprisingly, I enjoyed it. But a few hours later, when I awoke, I had a cold and a temperature of 102. Mabel was all for staying on until I felt better, but as we had reserved our places on the train to Paris, I deemed it worth the risk and all the discomfort to get a bit nearer England and home.

Most of the journey meant nothing to me; I was in a semi-coma and interested only in sleep. Paris was covered in snow when we arrived, and Mabel instantly tucked me into bed and sent for a doctor. He arrived in less than a quarter of an hour, a fussy little man with a black leather bag that made me think his main occupation was midwifery.

"Ah!" he ejaculated on catching sight of his patient; and that was the only utterance we were to understand until his departure. He sounded my chest, looked long and hard at my tonsils, and then lapsed into an ecstasy of French that was punctuated with confident gestures towards the out-of-doors. He was a pleasant enough chap, and Mabel tried hard to speak a word or two in his own language. Pointing at me and then towards the window, she said: *"Promenade?"*

For a second he looked puzzled; then suddenly shot back: *"Non!"*

Mabel looked back at me. "You've got to stay in, Pickles!" she said. After the doctor had left she decided to go out shopping. "I'll get you something to read."

The book she brought back was from the English section of one of the big bookshops in the heart of Paris. It had a bright cover and a cheery title, but it was the most pornographic publication I have ever seen. Oddly enough,

however, my temperature went back to normal soon afterwards.

When the doctor came again he beamed his pleasure
on both of us and again came out with a torrent of French
that meant nothing. We smiled and nodded our heads and I
shrugged my shoulders like a Frenchman.

The doctor prepared to leave, waving his little black
bag in farewell. He grabbed the door handle and called:
"Bonjour, monsieur, madame!"

A slight bow. Then he tugged at the handle. It came
away in his hand. We all laughed. "Ah!" he exclaimed.
"Laurel and 'Ahrdy!" For the first time we were on common
ground!

Paris in the winter was even more inspiring than I had
imagined, and more cosmopolitan than London, with its
babble of Continental languages, its bookshops gaudy with
fantastic covers, its bearded young men wearing sandals and
ladies wearing moustaches. We strolled about the boulevards,
revelling in the spacious planning and the sharp air.

I noticed that the streets were perfumed and the shops
stacked with luxury goods. We finished up at the Folies
Bergère and walked back to the hotel along the crowded
pavements at a time when most people in Britain were in bed.

"The only girl I liked among that lot," I remarked to
Mabel, "was the one with a skirt on!" The following
morning, as we were going for the train, Mabel glanced at
her watch and said there was just time to have one last look
at the shops. Soon we were in one of those lavish lingerie
stores where the stock as well as the highly manicured and
over-carefully made-up brunettes is scented.

Across the counter two women were examining the
goods with all the uninhibited concentration of housewives
in Halifax market. One of them fished out a piece of
shimmering silky material, waved it in the air, beckoned to
a third woman and shouted: "Ee, Alice! Drawers 'ere just
suit thee!"

As I remembered all this, I stood looking out of
the window of Donald Stephenson's office. Below, in
bustling Piccadilly, Manchester, they were running for

their lives for their buses across the broad square, thousands
of people on their way home after the day's work.
Many of them had never seen Paris and some would
never get the chance. As the traffic lights changed, the
cars and lorries and buses piled up in deep ranks and a
small army of men in mud-spattered clothes crossed in front
of them.

I wondered whether they were really concerned about
the sort of programmes that were broadcast, whether among
them were men who mourned the passing of Tommy
Thompson. If a public opinion poll were taken in that
moment of life, an instantaneous picture of the outlook of
the man-in-the-street, would it show that folk cared whether
the B.B.C. regions got more autonomy, or less?

Somehow, I felt slightly discouraged. It was important
that the individuality and independence of regional life and
accents should be preserved and reflected by the B.B.C. It
was one of the fundamental freedoms, and I wanted to
explain to all those preoccupied people on the pavements
below just what they stood to lose by the B.B.C.'s policy of
standardizing accent and outlook.

Here were folk doing similar jobs and working the same
hours as others in Scotland, Wales and the Midlands. They
were part of the same nation and shared the same traditions
and aspirations. The economic dangers of peace and the
physical dangers of war came alike to Jock, Tyke and Taffy.

Yet between each was a boundary of character and
experience, of habit and circumstance, out of which came
the variety of qualities that make a people strong. I thought
of the wealth of humanity within the borders of the North
Region; of the weavers, the dockers, the wool merchants
and the steelworkers; of boilermakers and blast furnacemen;
of market traders and knockers-up; of the first-class schools,
such as Manchester, Bolton and Blackburn Grammar Schools,
Leeds Modern and the technical colleges where our industries
were insured with human brains and ingenuity, against the
hazards of the future.

This work-blackened north, as rugged and enduring as
its people, had more to it than mills and machinery. Looking

down on Piccadilly, I knew that here was the centre of a distinctive morality and culture and way of life that had too few spokesmen; for there were thousands of Londoners who not only had never seen Paris, but had never set eyes on the north. Many of them believed that the north (a vague acreage beyond St. Albans) was dirty, ill-kept, ugly and forlorn; a wasteland where only bad taste and harshness thrived.

How different was the real north! On my last visit to Lancashire, a few weeks earlier, I had gone to Burnley to present certificates of merit to nurses at a big local hospital.

When we drew in at the main entrance, a group of them gathered round the car. They were trim and tidy, with blue-and-white uniforms that would have been a first-rate advertisement for the best soapsuds. Their faces were full of sympathy and intelligence; and in their laughter was a tuneful reassurance that the best in human nature had not been lost with earlier generations.

"What a grand lot they are!" I said to Mabel as we stepped out among them. To me they stood for all that was good and worth while not only in the world and the nation but in the north.

In the heart of industrial Lancashire these girls, many of them still under twenty-one years old, had worked on their mission of mercy, and now they were come to collect their testimonials.

Suddenly, like a yacht in full sail, emerged the matron, a Scot, a woman of action who was admired and respected by every one of the nurses under her. "I won't have you behaving in this way!" she called. And that was the end, for the moment, of our boisterous welcome!

I remembered that on one of my visits to wounded troops in a northern hospital an ex-paratrooper had explained how much he appreciated the gentleness of the nurses who daily changed the plaster dressing round his middle.

"They pull the old plaster off so delicately I hardly feel it, though I'm a bit tender round here!" he said. I recalled his remarks when I made my speech to the nurses. In all seriousness, for I was basing the remark on what the paratrooper had told me, I told them: "There's nothing

like a nurse for making you comfortable in bed!"
There was a gust of laughter. The matron was laughing,
and so was Mabel. I had expected dead silence. But there
was an even greater response when I said: "Nurses are born
and not paid!" That, from my point of view, was no
meaningless joke, for I really believed that nurses who
sacrifice so much and to whom humanity owes more than it
can ever repay in terms of tolerance and kindness, deserve
much better wages.

These thoughts and memories flashed through my mind
as I looked out from Donald Stephenson's window over
Manchester.

I heard Mabel's words, "Don't you think it's time we
were off?" and then we were in the narrow passage leading
from the studios where, sixteen years before, I had nervously
entered Broadcasting House, Manchester, for my first
audition. I remembered the "No Smoking" notice on which,
year in and year out, I had made my mark. The ritual started
in 1935, when I turned the card round and wrote: "January,
1935—Wilfred Pickles." In January, 1936, I repeated the
autograph, and again in 1937, 1938 and 1939. Only in 1940
did I discover that the finger-marked and dust-stained sign
had gone for good.

Through those years were embroidered the colourful
patterns of great broadcasts, worked in sound by writers with
poetry in their souls and by producers and artists with the
vitality of Lancashire and Yorkshire in their voices. Perhaps
there would be a resurgence of this distinctive culture when
television was thriving from Manchester to Newcastle and
Hull to Carlisle; perhaps the men in the north, with their
hard-headedness and far-sighted outlook, had made up their
minds that sound radio was obsolete.

Somehow, I could not believe that this was the reason
for the demise of northern broadcasting, but it was a possible
explanation. The problem of the future of radio in the north
was still troubling me when Mabel and I got back to Disley.
It was a crisp evening and the clouds had made way for a
pale blue sky.

"Come on," said Mabel. "I'll play you at snooker!"

"Three blacks?" I offered.

"Three blacks," she agreed.

So, with dusk beyond the windows, we switched on the light of our new billiards-room and chalked our cues. Here was the proudest of my possessions, the dream of my boyhood, an ambition realized! I owned a full-size billiards table made by Riley's, of Accrington!

"I'm going to have one," I used to promise myself as a boy. And I always knew it would have to be made by Riley's; no other would do.

No, not even a Burroughs and Watts would have satisfied me. I wanted to see that plate near the "D" end with the Riley's mark on it. It was part of my life plan, and in some way linked with my childhood in Essex Street, Halifax.

Mabel "broke off," which reminded me of the snooker player who challenged a Yorkshireman to a game. The Yorkshireman won the toss and his opponent had to break. This left the silent Yorkshireman an opening and he went on to clear the table.

The challenger looked astonished and said: "Let's play again!"

Once more he lost the toss and the Yorkshireman went right through to the black.

"I'll tell you what," said the challenger desperately, "I'll play you for a pound!"

The Yorkshireman put on an expression of worldly wisdom. "Not likely," he retorted. "I haven't seen thee play yet!"

My worries drifted away in the cigarette smoke that curled under the powerful table lights. This was relaxation; everything depended on that colourful array sitting on the green baize, and I had to be at my best to beat Mabel and her three blacks.

I have always delighted in snooker; but the quality of my play shows no signs of a misspent youth; I am not good enough for that. As for the professionals like Joe Davis, whom I like as a man and admire as a great player, I would rather not see them; for I always come away dissatisfied with my own game and being dissatisfied makes me determined to do better. And when I am desperately determined at snooker, I play abominably.

Mabel (with three blacks) is a worthy opponent; but I believe snooker is a game for four men with their sleeves rolled up to the elbows, their braces showing and with four pints of beer near their scoreboard. The thicker the drifting smoke under the lights the better the atmosphere.

I have played snooker in country houses and city pubs, miners' institutes, youth centres and the Albany Club, and in most of these places when the black is potted from a difficult angle, the cues are thumped like a drum-beat on the floor, and the wit of the party never fails to come out with his original compliment: "Give 'im the money, Barney!"

▪▪

CHAPTER NINE

Tuesday week

> *"The rolling English drunkard*
> *Made the rolling English road,*
> *A reeling road,*
> *A rolling road,*
> *That rambles round the shire.*
> *And after him the parson ran, the sexton and the squire;*
> *A merry road, a mazy road, and such as we did tread*
> *The night we went to Birmingham by way of Beachy Head."*

CHESTERTON'S LILTING LYRIC BUZZED AROUND IN MY MIND as Mabel and I coasted along the winding Pennine road to Yorkshire. Here was the north in all its rugged grandeur, where the blunt hills met the clouds; a raw and invigorating no-man's-land between the two great Roses' counties.

The words of the old man in the local at Disley came back to me: "Yorkshire! Yon's t'best road, by way of Manchester. Everybody knows it's best way!" But we had not followed his directions, and instead had taken the route through Hayfield to Glossop, where we had joined the Sheffield road.

It was a queer way to be going back to London; but, having come north in the middle of our holiday, we had decided to look up a few old friends in my native county, call on my mother and father and two brothers in Halifax, and visit the children's orthopaedic hospital at Thorpe Arch, a few miles out of Leeds.

"The day we went to London Town by way of Bill and Fred. . . ." This was the morning and the place where poetry might be born; the great Pennine hills with their gradients and greenery, their stubborn stone walls built goodness-knows-when, their little grey homes tucked into the folds of marginal farms.

This was the landscape that has never failed to invigorate me, and it occurred to me that if I were ever asked my own *Have a Go!* question, the one about the simple things in life that give people a thrill but cost nothing to enjoy, this would be my answer. The Pennine Way, bleak, rocky and defiant; part of the backbone of England, with its grim jutting rocks, its benty grass, nettles and babbling streams.

I thought of the streaking autobahns of modern Germany, of the mighty highways of America, great livid scars of concrete cutting the countryside in a dull, efficient gesture to speed. They were mean things in contrast to the Pennine road, as tawdry as chromium snack-bars in the shadow of a cathedral.

I could understand the feelings of that wonderful old lady of Beverley, in Yorkshire, who only a few weeks earlier had appeared in *Have a Go!*

Grey and serene, she was ninety-one and blind, and had been a schoolteacher for more than half a century. "Have you had any desire to live anywhere else?" I asked her.

She shook her head as the audience went silent waiting on her words. "Not out of this country—not away from my England."

Now, on the Pennine hills, I appreciated her outlook; and the thought came to me that time counted for little in this immortal countryside where the simple ways of life were still in vogue and men struggled to bear their environment and to wrest food and shelter from the harsh hills.

Here was reality and here were the dependable folk, their lives uncomplicated by ambition and changing fashions. I wondered what was going on behind those sturdy walls, in the cottages with the smoke curling from stone chimneys. Perhaps I knew, for family life and individual skills still thrived in these parts.

Suddenly from afar, we spotted the giant mast of Holme Moss stabbing out from the moor. This was the only ugliness we had seen, a spire of steel searing the landscape like some garish scarecrow. I wondered whether its intrusion would ever be justified, whether it would bring beauty into the homes of millions of northerners once they had found the money to buy their television sets.

We talked of all the tinsel glamour which the B.B.C. had broadcast in the name of entertainment on television; of the pretentious pictures that stamped the medium as a mirror of the West End rather than as a means of popular public communication; of the toothpaste smiles, the dressing-up, the stagey artificiality that marred programmes and showed that, instead of learning from the experience of the men and women who had adapted and built up the whole structure of sound radio in Great Britain, the television chiefs were falling into the same traps and troubles as the B.B.C. had scrambled through in its first twenty-five years.

"The trouble is that they're trying to standardize expressions and smiles just as they tried to standardize English," I said.

My own serious début in television was a chance, I had thought, to put ordinary folk in front of the camera just as *Have a Go!* had given them the freedom of the microphone. I felt they would bring some overdue sincerity to the television screen and a lesson to those who saw no farther than Leicester Square and the smart set when it came to finding personalities for the medium.

They brought the sincerity all right, and I had encouraging letters from thousands of viewers in the London and Midland areas who were anxious to see more uninhibited folk from the homes, factories, farms and fisheries of this prolific island. But the lesson was lost, for before I quite knew what was going on my original idea of presenting the people to the people on television, just as I had been trying to do over the air for so many years, had been intellectually anaesthetized into a half-hearted documentary about places with problems.

What had begun as a programme called *At Home* was suddenly transformed into a couple of soap-boxes with me in between. Even this, I felt, was better than continuing the tradition of gaudy nonsense for which the men at Alexandra

ting 'em on.

Getting 'em off.

overing.

Reminiscing.

Wilfred as Willie Mossop in the stupendously successful Blackpool run of *Hobson's Choice*.

Palace had won an unenviable reputation; but I was convinced that it was not right. Every place had its problems, lots of them; they were to be found in every city and hamlet in the country; but it was one thing to let these problems roll naturally off the tongues of the ordinary folk in studio interviews, and quite another to go along to these places with problems already decided at television headquarters.

There were man's battles against the elements and the "slings and arrows of outrageous fortune"; there were couples falling in love and having families; there were others falling out of love; and there were the problems over schooling and health and faith. But the B.B.C. chose instead "specific problems"; and it was like attempting to focus the West End and giving only a galaxy of gags and gang-shows. For there are people struggling to make ends meet in the West End just as there are in West Bromwich; journalists who have ventured south to earn their living; models, architects, artists and engineers, all with problems that have nothing to do with the bright lights.

If the B.B.C. want to examine one overriding social or economic problem in one particular area, let them get a feature-writer to work on it for them; let them produce the economists, politicians, town councillors and town planners, all the specialists who know exactly what is wrong and what is being done about it.

But I say it is misusing the qualities of ordinary folk, and losing much of what they have to offer to television in the shape of their personalities, to try to canalize what they say into one avenue of conversation. In any case, problems are as big as the individual makes them and it is much more important to one town councillor that the Waterworks Committee takes over some allotments than it is to another who is more interested in seeing a new school built. Asparagus may be more important than arithmetic, depending on which committee you belong to.

Once, when my own biggest problem was my health, I was sent by my doctor to a specialist who diagnosed something completely different to the complaint suspected by the general practitioner. I called on my own doctor and told him.

He rested his stethoscope on his chest, sat back and chuckled: "Ee, we do have fun, don't we!"

We saw the problem differently. But we were both actors, as most people are at heart. There is a streak of exhibitionism in nearly everybody, and once ordinary folk have thrown off their shyness they often surprise themselves by their capacity to amuse and entertain and to say interesting things like the so-called celebrities.

I often used to wonder what made men give up their leisure to sit on council committees until midnight instead of staying by their own firesides teasing the cat or playing "homeward bound" with the children. Having seen them at council meetings I realize that it is for gratification of the urge to show off that many go into public work.

I glanced towards Mabel. She was still taking in the scene and suddenly pointed towards a man in dungarees and black leather leggings. He was a dry-waller, building walls without mortar, and I felt proud that I was one of the dwindling number of craftsmen capable of doing this job.

"It's becoming a lost art," I said. "What a chance for television to film him on the job!"

I reflected on the days when I had tried to persuade the B.B.C. to record for posterity the vanishing dialects and folk-songs and stories which enriched the life of the regions of Britain. There was little enthusiasm for the idea at first; but gradually some effort was made to capture these sounds for all time. I knew that television would not regard this as a precedent, for what radio does today the men of television studiously avoid doing tomorrow, so determined are they to prove that television is new, fresh, different and owing relationship to no other medium, least of all sound radio.

It surprised me to find so many television directors and administrators gripped by a common contempt for what they refer to as "blind radio." "Blind it may be," I once told a television producer, "but it has shown Alexandra Palace the path to take. New medium my foot!"

During my television series, both the *At Home* programmes and those devoted to *Places with Problems,* I could never quite get used to the smug superiority of the studio staff towards their brothers in the less fashionable centres of the B.B.C. It seemed odd that these people could put on such airs when their programmes were so indifferent. Much of their light entertainment would have been hooted off any stage between the Palladium and the City Varieties in Leeds; and Mabel and I had spent many an evening in our London flat reading after switching off our television set in disgust.

The attitude of these lofty men of television was rather pathetic and reminded me of the typical old trouper who got the slow hand-clap and mistook it for genuine applause.

Perhaps it was because I had sensed this state of mind among the men of television that I so enjoyed the way a Yorkshire fisherwoman stole the show in one of our programmes. Dinah Theaker had seen men go down to the sea in ships for more years than most of the cameramen and lighting assistants and production men around her had been alive; she had a philosophy that had been nurtured through hours of meditation in her village home within the sound of the North Sea breakers.

It gave her strength and fresh outlook that made her indifferent to the fuss and excitement in the studio around her. I believe there were people among those present who mistook this casual attitude to the modern miracles that make up a television station for lack of imagination. How wrong they were! It was her values that made Dinah strong; her values and her appreciation of human nature.

"Here we are," said Mabel, "Huddersfield." We were dipping into the woollen town, a busy centre of industry known all over the world for its wool and Huddersfield Town; but, for me, important also for its famous Rugby League team, with its shades of the greatest centre of all time, Harold Wagstaffe. Huddersfield, one of those towns where family life is so obviously the main social factor and where houses are kept spick and span and have the warm, secure, homely atmosphere which is at the very root of our freedoms and way of life! Like Halifax, Huddersfield is full of memories for me; of Saturday afternoons on the rugby

ground, of days in the sun with a trowel or a hammer and
a pitching tool; of the most dour Yorkshire folk I have ever
met. I remembered my first job as a building apprentice
was out on Burnley Road; and as I had so often promised to
show Mabel the old manor house on which I had worked
at that time, we made a detour in order to see it.

There it was, grey and sturdy as a rock, with its old stone
and slate roof and its mullioned windows, a house made to
last. It was also, in this moment, the focal point of my early
youth. I saw myself earnestly helping the skilled men with
the mortar and the dead-weight stones, climbing ladders and
looking down and coming to the awful conclusion that I had
no head for heights.

It was on that job that I came to meet and like the
elderly foreman, Frank Bleazard, who was full of tips and
wrinkles and was gifted with a dry sense of humour. Once
we were working together in the posh part of Halifax and,
as usual, I was on about the stage and actors.

"Henry Baynton's here this week with his Shakespearian
company," I said excitedly.

"Oh, ay?"

"I'm going to see them at least twice."

"Ay?"

"You know, it's possible Henry Baynton himself might
walk this way—he's staying round here!"

Frank chipped a piece of mortar off a used brick, looked
round at me and grinned. "Ay?" he said.

Later that morning he called me round from the other
side of the house, nodded towards a little man wearing a
shabby overcoat and a muffler and bowler hat who had just
walked round the corner, and said: "Hey, Wilfred—here's
Julius Caesar!"

Halifax was at work and the shopping centre almost
deserted as we drove in. I was anxious to show Mabel the
covered market, a great stone shed with a glass top which
always thrilled me as a boy. In some queer way, it held all
the mysteries of the universe between its walls and drew me
inside like a magnet.

It seemed much bigger to me in those days, an

adventurous world beyond my own home and street, a centre of commerce where men and women bought and sold everything from meat to books and where tradesmen with strong eyes and voices shouted their wares under the light of flare burners that sizzled above their heads. A great draughty place it was, too, and often enough I have used some buxom housewife as a wind-breaker while, open-mouthed and over-awed, I watched the butchers spellbinding the shoppers with their cries: "Nice little bit 'ere, lady!" or "It's all good, every piece!"

I used to look up at the swaying carcases, strategically hooked to keep the draughts off the burners, and wonder why people ate meat at all. Not all this mass of flesh was bought, for there always seemed to be a considerable shield of mutton round the market perimeter. Inside, in the centre of the hall, which had a strong smell, all its own, made up of funeral wreaths, meat, flowers and wet sawdust, was Moore's toffee stall. There you could stand watching the girls, wearing white celluloid cuffs, as they broke up slabs of toffee with small hammers.

Nearby was the most curious stall of all, where they displayed white waxed flowers encased in glass. This symbol of mourning contrasted with the stall a few yards to its right along the cold, sanded floor of the hall, where you could buy babies' jackets. The market summed up the whole of life's story, from the cradle to the grave; it could feed the stomach as well as the mind, and I have bought most things, from meat pies and razor blades to a set of Minton china, from its traders.

"Like a razor, like a lance!" I used to gaze in wonder at the cheapjacks, the Saturday invaders of the lower market adjoining the slaughterhouse, as they put on their performances to sell knives and cutlery. Extravagant, cheeky, over-confident, they were the commandos of commerce who used to make me late home for dinner by their oratory.

Even the smell of blood that came horribly from the slaughterhouse was forgotten as they tiraded about the qualities of the goods they had for sale. I would stand by their stalls; then go back into the glass-domed hall to gaze rather fearfully into the dim, mysterious cafés where people went for tea and meat pies. The only special dish they served was "baked beans on your pie."

These cafés were as dramatically puzzling as the little recesses alongside each market stall where the holders would disappear between customers. What did these corners conceal? What went on there? I often wondered, but never really found out. And if I had seen for myself, I doubt whether I should have been satisfied; it might well have been disappointing to see the straw-hatted and aproned traders doing nothing more exciting than counting their takings or signing bills or having a nap.

It was in Halifax Market Hall that I bought my first book. It was *Bell's Elocutionist,* and it cost me half a crown. How to Express Yourself, it pronounced; and then went on to describe, in words and line drawings, those fantastic gestures of hands and eyes and shoulders that were once mistaken for classic demonstrations of making oneself understood.

I remember walking slowly home with the book open at the pages explaining fear and despair. Even at my age, the gesticulating figure which was supposed to represent fear looked like a humorous caricature.

As Mabel and I walked through the hall, it was quiet except for the rattle of cups and saucers and, here and there, snatches of intimate conversation about "your Annie still being in t'market"! But for me it was filled with the ghostly sounds of thirty years and more ago.

Fashions had changed and so had the smells, but there was still the familiar bookstall where I bought my first lessons in elocution; the pea-and-pie saloon where folk used to stuff themselves with meat pies, splashings of gravy and a glass of dandelion and burdock. There were still, too, those furtive entrances to adjoining pubs, almost like priest holes in the market building.

"Still the same sort of swing doors and the same draughts," I told Mabel. We were passing a clothing stall where a woman in black and early middle age was ostentatiously holding up a girl's dress to the filter of light stabbing through the shimmering dust of the place. Evidently she had been there some time, for a little woman in spectacles came breathlessly to the stall holding a pot of tea in one hand and a daily newspaper in the other, and exclaimed: "I'm sorry, luv. Just been to get this!" She nodded towards the teapot.

A gust of cold air caught us as somebody pushed open a swing door. I wondered if Fortnum and Mason, or Marshall and Snelgrove, or Swan and Edgar had ever been up to Halifax Market. And what would the tail-coated salesmen of Bond Street think of this emporium of trade? What a treat to bring one of them into this world where the customer could quite easily be wrong, where frankness rather than smooth diplomacy was the technique of the seller!

Many years earlier, Mabel and I had called in a Liverpool market to buy a few things for a woman we knew who was trying to set up house. We were just beginning to get on our feet and had a few shillings to spare. We picked up a few kitchen items, some pictures and an ornament or two, and as the stallkeeper was parcelling them up, she regarded us with that coy, knowing glance beloved of so many northern women and, with her head tilted slightly sideways, said: "Are you getting a little home together?"

I was still thinking of the market hall and its Arabian Nights background as later, having made our various calls, we drove out of my home town towards Leeds. We passed street after street that I had known well; huddles of houses collectivized under some such name as Rhoda Street or Mary Street, where men and women had been born, done their courting, got married, had families of their own and who had become as familiar a part of the scene as the masonry, the corner shop and the soot-grimed walls. What I had always dreaded as a youth, and possibly without knowing it as a very young child, was to let my life go by in such surroundings. The thought of an interminable round of work from eight to five in town and the evenings spent in a house in one of these obscure streets was like a nightmare. But there were people who found happiness in such an environment.

I once knew a couple, who lived in William Henry Street in one of our big northern mill towns, and who were ideally happy.

They had grown up just a few streets away and they told me confidentially: "We were lucky to get our house in William Henry Street. Bit of influence, you know! Mr. Jackson spoke for us!"

I have often wondered who these people are who "speak" for others, and whether they are as influential as they like to think. As far as I remember, nobody has ever spoken for me; and if I ever buy anything, or sell anything, or acquire anything, it is always at a price favourable to the other party. "If you'd only come a month sooner, now . . . !" or "We've got that many of these things we can't get rid of 'em!" I always buy at the wrong time, sell at the wrong time, and lose money on every deal. Much as I would like to be one, I would never make a market trader.

We stayed in Leeds just long enough to book in at the Queen's Hotel in the heart of the city—an expensive, expansive and altogether superb place with white walls that almost convince you that nobody could ever commit original sin within miles of it. Then we set out for Thorpe Arch, a village set delightfully in that fertile land east of Leeds.

It is one of our favourite calling-points, for it was there, in the village school, that I did my first broadcast with children after the death of our son David. John Salt, that brilliant young man whose career in radio held such promise, spent much of his youth in Thorpe Arch and was buried there. It was John who urged me to do that difficult broadcast. "It will do you good to mix with other children now," he counselled. I realized how right he was, and since that time I must have done hundreds of programmes with boys and girls and visited the orthopaedic hospital almost as often as I have been into Yorkshire.

I have sometimes advised people who are not contented with their lot to call on the youngsters at Thorpe Arch, many of whom have been on their backs for most of their lives. They might find inspiration in the courage of these boys and girls and the devotion and idealism of the nurses who care for them.

Happiness gleams from every cot and corner in this airy, cheerful hospital, where the battle for life and hope among the afflicted young is being won by the spirit of a handful of young doctors and nurses and assistants. Whenever we call, Mabel and I usually have the car loaded up with gifts sent to us for distribution among invalid children. This was no exception, and as I got out I pointed towards the back seat. The matron, a friendly woman in early middle-age who has the vigour and outlook of someone twenty years younger, clasped both hands to her cheeks in an expression of surprised delight.

"They're mostly from ordinary people who don't even want to be thanked," I explained. "There are more kind folk in the world than the other sort."

On the veranda above us, in a row of cots and beds, were the kids, who sensed they had a visitor. Soon we were among them, talking about toys and ice-cream and the burning topic of getting better. I remembered the attractive little girl who, on our last visit, had been reading a book by means of a special contraption that reflected the reading matter above her, on to the ceiling. It had been sent from America. "Please," she said, "will you thank the American Red Cross when next you go over there!" It was spontaneous, it was sincere and it was a lesson in values. I never forgot her words and I never forgot her expression as she spoke them.

Out of the mouths of the very young comes so much wisdom and wit. I told Matron two stories I had heard in London. A class of boys and girls were being shown Easter pictures of Christ on the Cross when one puzzled youngster, who remembered being shown the infant Jesus' picture the previous Christmas, piped up: "Who's that?"

"Jesus Christ," explained the teacher.

"My!" the little boy retorted, "hasn't he grown since Christmas!"

The other story was about a five-year-old girl and her three-year-old brother who were playing at "Mr. and Mrs.

Brown." They knocked at the door of a neighbouring house where a friend of their mother lived.

"Yes," she said. "What is it?"

"We're Mr. and Mrs. Brown. We've come to see you," said the little girl.

"Come in," smiled the neighbour, appreciating their game and playing up, "come in and have a glass of milk."

Out came the cakes and the milk and the chocolate, and all through the little party the neighbour continued to address them as Mr. and Mrs. Brown.

Suddenly the little girl stood up and said: "Well, I am afraid we must leave now."

"Must you go so early, Mrs. Brown?"

"Yes," said the little girl, "I'm afraid we must; you see, Mr. Brown has wet his trousers!"

I told Matron I thought it was time somebody set about the job of collecting children's sayings into a book.

There is certainly an abundance of material for some bright editor willing to undertake the necessary research. Perhaps the richest of all the stories I have heard about the antics and remarks of the very young concerns a young business man who was doing fairly well in the world and had started entertaining his "contacts" at home. One night he and his wife packed off their four-year-old daughter, Jane, to bed and welcomed half a dozen guests. Suddenly, in the middle of the proceedings, the little girl burst into the lounge with her lips set tight and her nightdress dripping wet.

"Whatever has happened to you?" asked her father.

Jane looked about her, gazing at each of the visitors in turn, and said: "I don't know which gentleman left the seat up, but I just fell in!"

Going back to Leeds from Thorpe Arch, Mabel and I talked about children, those we had met at the hospital and those who turned up in *Have a Go!* Mabel started to chuckle.

"Do you remember little Mary on the mining tour?"

Yes! There she stood, a ten-year-old who looked seven, with a pretty Irish face, blue eyes, long hair in ringlets and beautiful dark eyelashes. She was rather quiet, but was anxious to be selected for our *Have a Go!* show in which I was to interview five children. That meant that seven had to be disappointed; so Mabel and I decided to ask them a few questions beforehand to find the best talkers.

The little girl with the Irish face was a lovely child, but she had nothing to say except yes and no, but said that she'd like to sing for me.

"All right, luv," I said. "Well, I'll have to see some of the others now!"

When we picked our five youngsters little Irish was not among them. Mabel went into the room at the back of the cinema and read out the names of those who would be taking part. The others filed out to their seats in the stalls. But not Mary; she stayed behind.

Mabel counted six departures, checked up, and spotted Mary. "I'm sorry, love, but you're not in the quiz! You can watch it from the front row."

Mary held firm. "Oh, I know I'm not in the quiz," she said innocently. "But I'm singing for Wilfred!" Mabel had not the heart to say any more, so we altered our schedule and included six children—and Mary sang for us, and sang beautifully.

It was in Bristol that a woman told me about her little boy who saw a report in the evening newspaper that "Wilfred Pickles is confined to his bed with influenza."

"What does confined mean?" he asked his mother, who answered as best she could. He pondered things over for a moment in front of the fire and then called out: "Well, Wilfred Pickles has had it then! Give 'im the money, Barney!"

What a humanizing influence children are! Talking about them brought back to mind one of the happiest, most hectic and tiring weekends Mabel and I have ever had. We had been to Much Wenlock with *Have a Go!* and there met a twelve-year-old lad; dark, curly haired and composed, with a calm disposition, who had won the affection of millions for the way he had spoken on the air.

It came out during the broadcast that he was at Dr. Barnardo's Home, and hundreds of people wrote to me asking if they could adopt him. The following day, Mabel was in the kitchen washing-up when she said: "How about inviting Carl here for a weekend?" So it was that Carl and his ten-year-old brother, Tony Plumb, arrived with their best suits and attaché cases at our London flat.

The city was a great gorge of a place to them, and they gazed in wide-eyed wonder at everything they saw. I believe they were somewhat disappointed to find that Mabel and I lived not in a broadcaster's mansion, with butlers and footmen, but a three-bedroomed flat with a sitting-room, kitchen and bathroom, and a key, not a flunkey, to let us in.

Whatever gave Carl and Tony the idea that people whose voices they heard coming out of a wireless set were wealthy, is something I would have liked to know more about, but there is no time to bother about trifles like that with the whole of London to see: Buckingham Palace, the Zoo, Broadcasting House and the Houses of Parliament and the waxworks—and, of course, the underground escalators!

For fully half an hour I rode up and down the long moving staircase at Oxford Circus, with Carl and Tony finding adventure and discovery in every second. I was quite thrilled myself. When we got back home, Mabel was toasting some crumpets under the grill. She came into the lounge to talk to us and we all got so involved in describing what Carl and Tony had seen that the crumpets were forgotten. Suddenly there was a smell of burning and she dashed back to the stove—too late!

One of the lads followed her into the kitchen and said: "Please, miss, I like them better burned than the other way!" It was a thoughtful gesture that touched us both. Carl and Tony stayed two nights and found as much to marvel at on the television screen as they had found in the heart of London. They kept creeping nearer and nearer the set until they were right on top of the picture and it must have seemed terribly out of focus.

They would come in wearing their pyjamas and sit on the rug as we all played "I Spy." It was a wrench for all of us when they left, but I have no doubt we'll all get together again quite soon.

In Leeds, the children were on their way home from

school as we drove through. They looked well and happy, full of life and energy, and in their rosy cheeks and laughter was all the reward any citizen could wish to have for the policy of his own generation in putting the youngsters first. We drove carefully past a point where an elderly man was waiting to shepherd a group of boys and girls across the road.

He waited until he had a substantial party and then set off, curbing the traffic and laughing through his moustache at the noisy throng around him. He was for all the world like some benevolent Pied Piper.

Back at the hotel, we rested for an hour, then scanned the menu with its high-sounding French names and wordy grandiloquence.

I looked across at Mabel. "Any ideas?"

She shook her head. I shook mine. "You know what I fancy?" she suddenly said. "A bag of fish and chips!"

"Harry Ramsden's?" I exclaimed.

"Harry Ramsden's!" she replied.

We rose, bowed to the waiter, who bowed back, and soon we were on the road to Guiseley, which not only houses Barney Colehan, his wife, Monica, and the two little Colehans, but also the man who is the supreme artist in the business of making fish and chips. How often have Mabel and I made a detour of several miles for no other reason than to sit in the car, with a bag of fish and chips apiece and the windows steamed up, and that lovely, battery, vinegary smell in our nostrils!

Harry Ramsden is a stocky, grey-haired chap with a smile like a sunrise over Ilkley Moor. He has a red face, a great business brain and a love of Yorkshire and fish and chips. I am something of an expert on this delightful dish; I know by the smell and the texture as well as the taste just how good the cooking is; and I can never resist a fish-and-chip shop once I get its scent. It has the same effect on me as aniseed has on a dog.

But this man Harry Ramsden is the "chipper" of all time. He has made a fortune out of the business he opened in a little hut on the site of his present elegant roadside restaurant-cum-café-cum-fish-and-chip shop. It thrives today on the custom not only of locals but of people who drive, walk or cycle miles for "a fish and three pennorth." Harry could sell out for thousands; he could sit back in luxury in the romantic capitals of the world living off caviare and sturgeon.

"Why do you keep on working, Harry?" I once asked this grand character.

"It's like this," he explained. "If I sold up I wouldn't be able to see the name 'Harry Ramsden' up there, would I? I've been down south, I've been to France and other places abroad. But I'm always glad to get back!"

Back to fish and chips and trout in the beck stream! Back to a sleepy Dales' village! Back to Hull or Halifax! It was Jack Jones who said of his native Wales: "It wraps itself round you like a blanket!" And it was Dorothy Una Ratcliffe who, in her poem "Yorkshire's Five," wrote so beautifully of Yorkshire:

"When I'se been by Tiber an' when I'se been by Seine,
Listenin' theer messages, I lang to hear agen
Secrets of home-watters, born amang moor-sedges,
Fallin' doon like sparklin' ale ower steean ridges.

An' when I'se been by Danube, an' when I'se been by
    Rhine,
Tryin' to onderstand 'em, my homin' heart 'ud pine
For t' music o' my ain becks 'at spring 'mang boggy peat,
Wheer lapwings cry an' moorlarks lift prayers sae pure
    an' sweet.

Missouri an' St. Lawrence, Volga an' Thames an' Dee,
All on 'em are varra fine, but niver t' same to me
As rivers 'at are singin' wheer my faither speech prevails,
A-crinklin' an' a-cranklin' doon my forsaken Dales."

Those words were written for men who love their native heath, men like Harry Ramsden of Guiseley.

■□

Wednesday week

OUR ROAD TO LONDON WAS PAVED WITH TOO MANY intentions. We planned to look up old and new-found friends in several towns and villages on the way down-country; but, as so often happens to ambitious hopes of this sort, they were largely unfulfilled. However, we managed a visit, off our route though it was, to that modern-age pit at Bolsover, where management and miners have confounded the sceptics and shown what can be done in an atmosphere of trust and happy human relationships.

After the lazy, sandy canyons of north Derbyshire, the pit scene comes sharp and harsh, with its row upon row of red-bricked miners' cottages and its gaunt slag-heaps scarring the landscape—immortal symbols of the toil of men and the aching anxiety of their womenfolk.

It all came back to me: all I had seen and heard on my tour of the collieries of Britain, all the guts and grim grandeur of the blackened men who had dug their way through years of tyranny and injustice and only now were getting something approaching a square deal. Their faces paraded before me—Jack, Bill, Bert and Harry—black, their helmets tilted, their eyes ringed with circles of cleaner flesh. Who, I wondered, could not be moved by the sight of such as these? Who would have the impertinence to grumble about the price of coal after seeing a shift of miners come up from the coalface?

Once, not so many months earlier, I had stood at a pit-head in South Wales and said in all innocence: "I'd like to see a tub of coal coming up!"

From behind came a calm, sing-song voice: "Well, go down and get it your bloody self!" The remark brought me

up with a jolt; but I bore no ill-will to the man who made
it. He was right. I believe everybody in Britain ought to be
told the same thing; for, if the miners were to refuse to dig,
I fancy we would all, quite soon, be burning logs or
perishing to death!

Now, seeing Bolsover again, the whole brave and tragic
tale of coal was brought to mind. As we drove up the curving
road towards the office, between well-kept lawns and flower-
beds, I recognized several of the men Mabel and I had met
when we called with a television unit to film sequences and
interviews for a *Places with Problems* programme. We had
stayed longer than we had intended on that occasion because
Bolsover had such a vital story of enterprise and achievement. It took me by surprise, for I must admit I knew only
of pit disasters and production difficulties, strikes and
troubles; and I took these things as the complete picture.

No sooner had we drawn up at the main entrance than
a handsome giant of a man appeared with hand outstretched.
In my television programme he had told me, in front of the
cameras, of his job as area manager of the East Midlands
Division of the National Coal Board; and had gone on to
explain, in layman's language, the Bolsover experiment
which had increased the output of coal with fewer miners
at work. At the same time it had made for goodwill between
the men who dig and those who organize. This composite
triumph of mining engineering and human relations was
born as an idea in this young man's mind, and he had the
courage to see it through into what it had become, a national
example, a method to be followed by the rest of the industry.

I found W. V. Sheppard, like so many really brilliant
specialists, to be a man with an infinite variety of interests.
Already, walking up the steps to his office that looks out over
the whole of the neighbouring pit district, he was talking
not about coal or miners or his tremendous experiment, but
about television programmes, newspapermen, and the
Festival of Britain. I could see why the miners thought so
much of this engineer who had served the old bosses and was
now putting heart and soul into his job as a public servant.

"You remember," he said, "when you were doing the

programme. My wife told me before I came to be televised:
'Don't forget to sit up straight!'"

"You did extremely well," I said.

'Shep' grinned. "I'm a miner," he chuckled, "not a
film star!"

In a corner of his office was a scale model railway truck,
the sort they use for carrying coal, with the name "Bolsover"
painted prominently on the side. It had been presented to
him by the miners he trusts so much that he had staked his
growing reputation on them. Their faith in him was obvious
in their acceptance of a system which made nearly half of
them redundant and meant that several hundred had to find
jobs at other nearby pits.

We got round to the subject of coal. "It's a matter of
breaking down the old suspicions, and understanding each
other and the country's position," he said.

"Do you prefer working under the present set-up to the
old one?" I asked him.

He walked over to one of the big windows, his hands in
his pockets, and said, quite simply: "We're getting coal for
England now!"

Here, I thought, was a man of responsibility, one of
those public officials who are so often maligned by ill-
informed critics; a man unknown outside professional circles
and the little community round the pits in this hard-working
district of Derbyshire. It seemed wrong that so much
brilliance and personal effort should have to remain con-
cealed; and I could not help feeling that here was a man
with far more personality, and who was much better endowed
intellectually, than many so-called celebrities in other walks
of life.

"How is the experiment going?" I asked him.

He flicked his head sideways, winked, made a confident
gesture with his hand and said: "Great. I've nothing but
admiration for those men down there. Nobody can expect
them to do any more. And there was Cresswell, you know!"

Cresswell! How clearly I remembered that awful
disaster when a whole village had to go into mourning.

"We're still clearing it," he explained. Soon we were

145

on our way to this pit whose name will always be on men's lips so long as the human race needs coal to keep life going. It was 'Shep' who showed me a tree standing in a patch of grass on a twisting lane at Cresswell. "A few nights before it happened, that tree was split by lightning, and one of the oldest inhabitants, they say, gave a warning: 'There'll be some sad hearts in Cresswell!'"

I had looked on as he spoke to officials and a miners' representative about the operations underground. He drew his hand across a plan of the workings, pointing out areas that were still dangerous, and emphasizing: "We're not going to risk one more life in this pit. It can't be hurried!" I wondered how this young man who thought so much of miners had been able to face up to the distressing job of telling waiting wives and families at the pithead on the night of the disaster that there was no hope. But that was what he had to do—after an exhausting spell with a rescue team in the foul air underground.

I believe he would fight to the end rather than see his miners let down in any way. The industry needs many more like him; men who understand people as well as the production problem. Perhaps his strength derives from his happy family life, for he has a charming wife and three delightful children, two boys and a girl.

One of his treasures is a blind girl typist, Betty Charlesworth, "who never makes a mistake, I assure you!" He took me in to meet her and I dictated a letter to test Betty's Braille shorthand and her astonishingly accurate typing.

On the way to Bolsover from Cresswell we had passed scores of miners, many fresh from the pithead baths, and all had signalled their recognition of the area manager. Occasionally he would drop down into second gear, crawl past them and call a greeting out of the window.

Now, as Mabel and I pushed on towards London, southeast to join the Great North Road, I turned down my side-window because of the heat from the engine and the early afternoon sun. "Imagine," I said to Mabel, "being down a pit swinging a pick in this weather!"

"It's time they got a lot more pay than they do," said

Mabel. "They ought to be excused paying income tax on a job like that."

"Remember that ten-year-old girl in South Wales?" I said. "The one I asked to tell me what she would choose if a fairy gave her three wishes."

"And she could only think of one thing."

I pictured her standing there, a trim, attractive girl in a neat print frock, with hair as black as coal, but with the lustre of diamonds in it. All she could say was: "Just for my daddy to come home safe—always!"

I thought of all the people I had heard making complaints about dirty coal, of those thoughtless critics who are too ready to condemn miners for betting, for drinking, for standing at streets corners and for "being cussed." If only I could round them up and take them to meet the men on the five-o'clock-in-the-morning shift. While the nation is still asleep, these men make their echoing way across the cobbles towards the lighted pityards, with their bottles of milk and their sandwiches. And in the tiny homes they have just left the housewives clear up, tidy the living-room, and maybe get ready for the next shift. Up in Easington, County Durham, I met a plump, jolly woman called Geneva Lavender, who had a grand sense of humour, and six sons down the pit as well as her husband.

She herself had started work as a pithead girl when she was only eleven years old, and recalled going on shift with her brother one drizzly, foggy morning in winter. They had to walk through a farmyard to reach the colliery, and Geneva tumbled slap into a manure heap!

"Well," recalled Geneva, "my brother says: 'Come on, we'd better get out of here!' But I says: 'I can't stir. I can't stir an inch, I'm up to my neck!'"

I couldn't resist it. "No wonder," I said, "no wonder they call you Mrs. Lavender!" Geneva laughed with all the uninhibited vigour of a woman who makes the most of every precious moment of happiness.

Life is one long hectic round of seeing her lads off, and I suppose that in the rare moments in which Geneva has time to worry she thinks of the dangers of mining. But this was not the Geneva Lavender who came up to the microphone on this happy night in County Durham.

"Of all the things in life that give you pleasure, what do you think you'd choose, luv?" I asked her.

Geneva grinned. "A Guinness!" she said.

As the laughter was subsiding I put another of my favourite questions to this wonderful woman. "If you had the chance to entertain somebody in your house, who would you pick?"

It came out pat. "Templegate, of the *Daily Herald*," she said. I explained, for those who took other papers, that Templegate was the *Herald's* racing correspondent.

"Look, Geneva," I said. "What do you dislike?"

Again that grin and a slight pause before the answer came out strong and without a trace of doubt. "A sour Guinness," she said.

This stopped the show. Fortunately, it was in a concert for the local folk and not in an official B.B.C. *Have a Go!* recording that this happened—and a good thing, too!

"Can you imagine," I said to Mabel afterwards, "the look of horror on B.B.C. officials' faces if that interview had gone over the air!" Advertising! What a tricky thing it is for the corporation to walk this tightrope of red tape, shouting about West End plays, films, books and gramophone records, but having to keep strictly silent about other "mentions," however innocent and true to life they may be.

Danny Kaye can bring in the Palladium six times in five minutes, as he did when I introduced and interviewed him in the B.B.C.'s *Festival of Variety* programme; but Geneva Lavender would be scraped off the recording for referring to Guinness. Even Templegate might well be a non-starter!

At least Geneva had no intention of giving a commercial company a free boost; but Danny's motive was plain even to a five-year-old. We discussed, very sketchily, the form the introduction and interview should take. There was no script, no hard-and-fast arrangement about dialogue, and he took me completely off my guard with his Palladium stuff. I felt that the whole thing was being grossly overdone.

It surprised me that the show, which was reported to

have a market value of something like £50,000, but for which the B.B.C. were rumoured to have paid not more than £20,000, went over at all. With all the big names, their temperaments and the cross currents set up by celebrities working together in a confined space, it was a wonder that we got through two hours without mishap.

I was sharing a dressing-room at the Playhouse Theatre, from which the broadcast was made, with Webster Booth, Frankie Howerd and Donald Peers. Franklin Engelmann, the announcer, suddenly burst in, excited and a little less smooth in appearance than usual, and appealed: "I need a dress waistcoat, I've just dashed over from B.H. and here I am without a waistcoat."

He looked at me. "Sorry, Jingles, I'm wearing a dinner jacket," I said. "But. . . ." I looked at Webster Booth through his dressing-table mirror. "Webster's might do!"

"Certainly," said the singing star. "Try it, old chap!"

It fitted near enough for most of the studio audience not to notice, but that was not the end of it, for, as the programme went off the air, "Jingles" had to go on the stage and make the closing announcement. This time there was no Webster Booth to come to his rescue. He had to face the microphone—and the audience—in his overcoat!

As Derbyshire slipped away under our wheels I thought of the Playhouse Theatre at Charing Cross on that fantastic Festival night and compared it with the Bolsover I had just seen. One was all perfumed make-believe; the other something real and down-to-earth; the stuff of serious drama, not variety. Both were, in their respective ways, important to the community; making people laugh or keeping them warm and comfortable, both were honourable services. Yet, while I had often contended that entertainers were not overpaid, in view of their lack of security, I also knew, after seeing the lives of the miners of Britain, that the men who get our coal are the worst rewarded section of the community. Their work has everything against it. Dirt, danger and discomfort mark mining out as the least attractive occupation in peace-time; a vital and terrible job for which there will never be a rush from the offices and factories, however many improvements are brought about in working conditions and wages.

At least there are lavatories in the theatre, and lights, too; daylight sometimes. If actors and actresses went on strike, it would be a sensation for the newspapers, but nobody would go hungry, the great industrial machine would not be halted, and the trains would still steam out of Euston and Paddington.

When the dockers come out on strike the authorities call in the soldiers to do their work. When the Smithfield meat porters leave their jobs, the R.A.F. can keep the butchers supplied. But you can't call in the Navy to dig coal. Either the miner does the digging, or the stuff stays underground.

No wonder he is so independent! This quality of detachment has grown out of his unnatural life burrowing in the dark seams underneath the earth. It is a legacy of the raw deals he experienced in the past when pit-owners lived in green and pleasant places nowhere near the mines that made their money. And what miserable indignities were inflicted on the miner in those days! During my journeyings round the pits of Britain I have heard a lot about the practice of compelling colliers to get the coal up with forks so that all the muck slipped through the prongs and stayed underground.

If the men were caught using a shovel they were fined a shilling. One old miner I met—he was seventy and still at work—told me how this miserable system was applied in his pit.

"Were you ever fined?" I asked him.

"Ay," he said. "T' week I were wed!"

Those were the days when every man who went down in the cage knew that if he did anything to displease the management there was a queue at the yard gate waiting for his job. No wonder the miner is suspicious, no wonder he keeps an eye on folk not of his kind. Now, thank God, man's humanity to man is beginning to assert itself and the miner and his family are no longer subjected to such affronts as were once practised.

But it will take years of work and understanding and many men like W. V. Sheppard, to balance the score.

Already, at Bolsover, the checkweighman system has gone: once, it would have been quite unthinkable for miners to give up this hard-won right to weigh their own output. They did not trust the bosses' men to do it; so they appointed and paid their own officials.

I have often wondered whether the young people growing up today, not only in the mining areas of Britain, but in the cotton towns and the shipbuilding ports and wherever the industrial system holds sway, appreciate the sacrifices and personal courage that have gone into civilizing our society. Abuses, and the degradation of human beings by a few, have not stopped by divine providence: they have been overthrown by little men with big hearts; men like the anonymous miners of Ashington, Northumberland, who set about the job of remedying an imposition on their freedom by building, like the great leaders of classical history, the places they wanted.

That is why today, the village of Ashington—the largest single mining community in the world—has two pubs and twenty-two clubs. This odd distribution of social centres arises from a decree by a duke who owned the land that not more than two pubs were to be put up in the village. So the miners showed their independence by going just outside his boundary and, by public subscription, building their own clubs. This determination to build a social life of their own is common to the majority of British miners who spend so much of their working lives alone, saying nothing, that they look forward to their off-duty hours above ground. In the mining areas today are youth clubs, dramatic societies and packed night schools. At one pit I visited I came across a man still in his dust and dungarees who was a great reader of Dickens: and he stunned me into respectful silence with as shrewd an analysis of the great writer's style as I am ever likely to hear.

Mabel and I drove along without saying much. The visit to Bolsover had revived so many memories, so many awful and inspiring real-life stories, and so many doubts in our minds about coal and the future of the men who get it, that we had virtually curled up within ourselves. I broke the

silence by asking for a cigarette. Mabel lit one for me and
as she fumbled for the lighter in the dashboard shelf an
envelope slipped out.

"What's that?" I said.

"Your Press Club subscription."

"Haven't I paid that?"

Club life has never meant a great deal to me, and I
wondered idly why I was a member of so many of these
meeting-places when I preferred to see people, for business
or socially, in the flat or at Broadcasting House. Only one
of these clubs gave me any real pleasure—and that was the
Maesteg Working Men's Club. In London I was a member
of the Savage, and the Albany with its subdued lighting and
air of opulence, but I felt more at home in that incon-
spicuous little club at Maesteg, where they play billiards in
a fug of smoke and sing as only the Welsh can sing.

One of the questions I have sometimes used in *Have a
Go!* is: "If when you're turning-in at night you can say,
'I've had a grand day today!' what would you have been
doing?" Well, if that question were shot back at me I would
have no hesitation in replying, "I've been listening to the
men of the Maesteg Working Men's Club singing 'Calon
Lan,' 'Cwm Rhondda' and 'Hen Wlad fy Nhadau.'"

To hear their voices raised in "Land of My Fathers"
sends a chill down my spine; for there is all Welsh history, its
poetry and sadness and all the nation's proud spirit in the
music.

It was early evening as we joined the stream of traffic
thronging in and out of London. "What do you fancy to eat?"
Mabel asked.

"Not particular," I said.

"You can have just what you like. That's a fair offer!"

"All right," I said. "Vegetable pie!"

This is one of my favourite meals and Mabel seems to
derive as much pleasure from making it as I do from eating
it. I joined her in the kitchen as she started to cook this
delicious supper. Into the dish went peas, beans and carrots,
with a slab of butter (most of our week's ration, I dare say)
on top, along with sliced potatoes. On went the electric oven,

and as Mabel made an inspection to see if the potatoes were browning and the crust baking, I slipped out, poured out a glass of beer for myself and a gin for Mabel.

"Cheers," I said.

"Cheers."

After a long journey, this is the drink we always enjoy most. Invariably we hold this modest cocktail party in the kitchen: you can have your "do" at the Dorchester, your sherry-sipping sessions, even your natter at the saloon bar. This is for me every time. Soon the meal was on the kitchen table, steaming pie with a lovely crisp crust and neat piece of cauliflower over which was poured white sauce with cheese in. I tucked in and so did Mabel.

"That," I said expansively, "was delicious."

"One of these days," said Mabel, "I'll teach you how to cook—then I'll be able to compliment you for a change!"

Feeling comfortably well-fed and rather tired we sat talking at our kitchen table, too settled even to move into the lounge with its armchairs and cosier atmosphere. I looked at my watch.

"Hey!" I said. "You know what the time is? Twenty-five past nine."

"Have a Go!" Mabel exclaimed. "Come on, then."

The announcer was just closing the programme before ours as we switched on. I sat back, then got up again almost in the same movement and walked round the room. I felt nervous, like an actor at a first night, as I always do when I listen to my radio recordings. I made notes in my mind as I picked out places where I might have been better by saying something or by keeping quiet, by making a humorous remark instead of a plain one, by encouraging somebody to carry on with a good personal story.

Mabel, as usual on these occasions, sat in her chair, laughing sometimes, nodding to me at parts of the programme that pleased her. For both of us, the voices in *Have a Go!* bring back visions of people we know; for us there is no speculation about what they look like. There are surprises sometimes, when a personality comes over delightfully when we had been convinced that his answers would sound rather slow and flat, and there are disappointments, too.

In this particular recording I burst into song, though I had forgotten this until my voice suddenly blossomed forth like an eager chorister's.

"Hold it, Pickles!" said Mabel.

Soon the talk was pouring out again. I put my head in my hands and Mabel resumed that faraway look. As the show finished I glanced towards her and said: "Not bad. The next might be better." Then the analysis started; with everything that was wrong and expendable and improvable coming out in a spate of criticism. This post mortem, held every Wednesday night wherever we are—in flat, house, dressing-room or even when we are staying with friends—always convinces me that nobody could have liked the show.

"I think," I said, "we ought to try a new——"

Suddenly, I noticed that dance music was now coming over the Light Programme. I went to switch it off. "Blow it," I said, "I won't!" I turned to Mabel. "Let's dance."

We jigged around like a young couple at the Palais de Danse, changing from fox-trot to waltz and shuffling around when it came to something more difficult and out of the ordinary.

"I'll tell you what, Pickles," said Mabel. "We've got a wonderful breakfast for morning!"

"How can you," I replied, "spoil this lovely tango with a mundane remark like that." But I was interested enough to steer us out of the lounge and into the kitchen.

"There." Mabel pointed to the guarantors of a bright morning—ham and eggs!

The B.B.C. changed its tune, the tempo quickened, the world seemed a gay and grand place to be in and we danced towards the bedroom. Then I went back to put out the refuse bin.

"Don't forget to switch the radio off," came Mabel's voice.

"Right."

"And the heating."

"Right."

"Have you locked the door?"

"I'm getting round to that any minute now."

"You won't forget the lights?"

"Never do."

"Not much!"

The mission completed, a tiring but pleasant day behind and a promising one ahead—full of people and voices and the sounds of everyday life that can seem so wonderful and entertaining when you are at one with the world—I settled down between cool sheets.

I switched off the bedside light. Through the window I could see a crescent moon and one searching star, brilliant and somehow reassuring, a living symbol of infinity and a reminder of the power and the glory beyond man's petty perimeters.

Even the roofs and chimneys of London, the skyline that had somehow survived after being battered, bombed and blasted, now looked fragile and shadowy against the bigger design of Night. But here was peace and here was hope; for London, for mankind, for the universe.

"Wilfred!" Mabel's voice came quietly.

"Yes."

"I've forgotten my glass of water."

"Good heavens!" I remonstrated rather like a Victorian father. "Twenty years and you still can't remember."

"I'm sorry."

"Very well," I said. "Let this be a lesson to you." Then I went for the water.

■□

CHAPTER ELEVEN

Thursday week

EARLY TO RISE, I WATCHED THE SUN COME UP OVER THE city on this, the brightest morning of our holiday. There was not a sound to disturb the dawn except, dimly in the distance, the hum of an aircraft on its way, perhaps, to another daybreak several hours away in some foreign capital.

In the skies, on the seas, were men and women restlessly crossing continents in their search for life. Yet here, I thought, in the quietened heart of London, was the perfect moment for those who chose to grasp it. This was a morning when peace and goodwill might be conceived, when mankind might find the values by which to adjust its own affairs.

It was a morning to stir the memory and I found myself thinking of those days as a schoolboy when I went out with my father on his pre-breakfast work; of the hilly lanes outside my valleyed town, bordering bright green fields fragrant with the smell of dew. We walked along together, saying little, thinking little, the proprietors of a bright new day.

Soon, we were on the job, amid the planks and ladders and sand-heaps and buckets, trowels and hods that were our stock-in-trade. From a nearby lane appeared another builder and a pasty-faced joiner who used to sit on a trestle eating a banana for breakfast.

But there was an hour's work before the first meal of the day.

"Morning."

"'Ow do!"

"Morning."

My father pulled out his watch. "Five to seven," he said. "Right. Let's make a point."

Everybody, including me, got down to business, and I
envied the men their freedom to work, for I was still a
schoolboy and this was no more than a bit of escapism,
"codology" as my father sometimes described my pretensions
as a builder. A few minutes before eight o'clock I would grab
the tea can and run down to the nearest house for a brew-up,
and when I got back we would all sit about with plain tea-
cakes and bacon-and-egg sandwiches and pint mugs full of
milkless tea. The larks were in full song, the cocks a-crowing
and the earth still wet with dew, that morning dew which
moved John Clare to write:

> "For every leaf that forms a shade
> And every flow'ret's silken top
> And every shivering bent and blade
> Stoops, bowing with a diamond drop."

What days those were that taught me to appreciate
morning! And how often since then have I made up my
mind to get into the early-rising habit, work before breakfast and take a walk before the streets are aired. I love the
morning the cockerels know, and condemn myself for not
making enough use of it:

> "Go to the ant, thou sluggard,
> Consider her ways and be wise!"

Mabel joined me at the window. "This is the sort of
morning to start your holidays," she said. "What's your idea
for today?"

"Something really original," I said. "I know, we'll
start the day right. We'll invite somebody to breakfast!"

"Breakfast?"

"They used to do it in the old days," I said. "Why
not?"

"Well, we've got some lovely ham and eggs."

"I know," I replied. "That's what I was thinking about."

The idea had slipped out almost unconsciously, but the
more I thought about it the better it seemed. After all,

breakfast was a much more appropriate meal to have with friends than lunch, when the guests feel embarrassed at having to leave so soon; or dinner, when they usually do not leave early enough. There are, of course, grumpy souls who are psychologically unable to find their sense of humour until eleven o'clock in the morning. For them a breakfast party would never do. So we decided our guests would need to have a similar sense of humour to our own and a meet-the-morning heartiness to enjoy a breakfast out.

"I know who," I said.

I telephoned Wilfred Greatorex and his wife Beryl, Lancastrians living in London.

"What's this?" said Wilfred. "A gag?" In less than a minute, however, I convinced him that it was perfectly serious.

I had first met this young journalist when he was with the *Yorkshire Evening News* at Leeds, and he had impressed me, and other B.B.C. people, as the liveliest man in the business. I liked his radio criticisms that appeared every Saturday; criticisms in which he not only laid into the B.B.C. but also gave constructive suggestions for the improvement of programmes. Once, I advised Lord Simon of Wythenshawe, Chairman of the B.B.C., to read these pieces, and a few weeks later Wilfred mentioned that the B.B.C. had asked him for a complete set.

We came across each other quite often in those days in the north, and at B.B.C. Press Conferences in Manchester he would get in first with an interview and be away in one of the studio telephones while the other newspapermen were still writing their stories.

I was not surprised when he moved to Fleet Street, for I am sure he has a bright future in journalism. I gave him one piece of advice which he seems to have taken: many of his articles were appearing under his by-line with the Christian name shortened to Wilf. I have never liked this. "It makes you sound like an American sports writer," I said.

Wherever I go, ninety-nine people out of every hundred call me Wilf; I am used to hearing it, but Mabel and the family always use the name in full.

Wilfred and Beryl drove down to our flat right away and the breakfast party went off so well that I wondered why hostesses do not make more of this meal instead of trying to fob their guests off with offers of the meal in bed. If there is anything that really frays my temper it is breakfast in bed. Our friends know by now that it is no treat for either of us; indeed, I always regard with suspicion any housewife who says coyly the night before: "I've got a surprise for you in the morning!"

What she really means is that she has schemed a method of keeping her guests out of the way while she straightens up the house. Sometimes, however, when Mabel and I arrive at some hotel late at night or in the early hours, we find breakfast served to us in bed by over-zealous hoteliers.

Once the waiter has gone, however, I slide out of bed and eat at the dressing-table. I have had too many irritating experiences, of crumbs clinging to the hairs on my chest, of marmalade down my pyjama jacket, ever to take breakfast in bed again. Give me an early breakfast every time, but let it be served either in the kitchen or in the dining-room; not in bed and not while I am still in my night-clothes.

We talked over breakfast about social habits and the conventions that made this very party unusual, then we got on to eccentricities and some of the more unconventional people we knew. The conversation was packed with names. There was Henry Moore, Priestley, Francis Laidler, R. W. Shawcross, editor of the *Yorkshire Evening News,* and a dozen others in politics, films, stage, radio and journalism. We finished up back in Lancashire and Yorkshire, reminiscing about people and places, the philosophy of the ordinary folk and their humour.

It occurred to me that one of the secrets of having a party is not to throw your net too wide and to make sure that those you are bringing together share the same ideas of what is amusing. It is the habit of many of the radio people I know to throw lavish cocktail parties that are more like revivalist meetings in Regent Street and all too often end up with bad feeling all round and a dreadful mess to clear away.

One of the main lessons I have learned from *Have a Go!*

is the variations that exist between groups of people—towards politics and entertainment in particular. The art of the politician and the entertainer, of anyone who must keep good relations with the public, is to find that narrow area of appreciation common to the majority, but even when it is located, there are no signposts to indicate where the unfortunate public figures may step into trouble or oblivion.

The safest way is to meet and try to understand as many people, of all classes, jobs, skills and accomplishments, nationalities, opinions and religions, ages and physical conditions, as possible, but at the same time to keep your circle of friends in small compass. The alternative seems to be confusion, endless argument, unpleasantness and strife—and certainly lack of self-assurance.

I have long since stopped worrying whether my programmes will please all the people; it is a pious hope, anyway. There are those who would not miss the quiz for anything and others who cannot abide it. This divergence of appeal and taste was summed up when I went to Glasgow soon after *Have a Go!* had become the B.B.C.'s top-listening programme. We had thought it would be a good idea to interview the students during the Glasgow University Rag week. Having seen something of rags in Manchester and Leeds, I was ready for prank playing and April tomfoolery, and while I sympathized with these affairs for their economic motives—raising money for hospitals and charities—I was not at all sure that even students should be allowed to inflict their extremes of humour on the rest of the community.

I have always regarded it as stupidly excessive to go knocking off policemen's helmets and dropping bags of flour on innocent members of the public; a form of perverted exhibitionism born of frustration.

We had been given the University Hall to produce the programme, and as I stood in the wings I could tell we had made a mistake. Those students were out to wreck the show! They howled and jeered, they whistled as soon as they were asked not to, they threw balls of paper, sticking-plaster, cigarette packets and other objects on the stage, and Violet Carson was given such a stormy time that I marvelled at her courage in sticking to her post at the piano. One of the university officials came to me, grabbed my arm and said: "Do ye think ye ought to go on with it?"

I nodded. "Above all else," I said, "they want to stop us. And the second thing they want is for me to lose my temper. I'm going to do neither. If they don't like it they can lump it, but this programme's going on!"

As I came out from the wings towards the microphone in the middle of the stage, they hooted, they catcalled and they heckled. This went on throughout the interviews. Millions heard it and millions were on our side. The students of Glasgow University responsible for the ragging condemned themselves by their own uncivilized noises.

For weeks afterwards, letters poured in from all over Britain, but mainly from Scotland. The cry that rose from this mass mail from over the Border was: "Don't think this is Scotland!" Naturally, I had no more associated the students' behaviour with the character of the Scots than I would think of blaming Londoners for the misconduct of the city's criminal classes. "Dear Wullie," wrote one brief gentleman from Aberdeen, "That was right wrong of 'em."

In Scotland, Mabel and I have found warm, generous people with a love of fair play and justice, folk who still regard courage as a great virtue. How well I remember that day up in wild and craggy Wester Ross, on the growling west coast of Scotland where we had gone to record one of those descriptive features in the *Pleasant Journey* series. Across the blue hills we had come to this outpost of our island, a settlement that had grown up where the Highlands meet the sea, and they made us right welcome.

The scene was raw and bleak in this almost forgotten village from which the minelayers crept out into the Atlantic during misty mornings in wartime. The roads were bad, the streets narrow and the sewage system was no more than a short pipe leading out into the sea. There were signs wherever one looked that Wester Ross had been left half a century behind, and I came to appreciate why there are Scots who blame Whitehall with such vehemence.

Our first night in the community was spent getting to

know its inhabitants, and I suddenly found myself face to
face with a brawny, middle-aged Scot who had obviously
taken too much drink. He thrust his nose between my eyes
and came out with a flow of bad language and abuse about
my nationality.

"English!" he said. "Tchaah!"

Noticing his condition, I let it pass, but suddenly the
door burst open and in came a real gust of a man. Over his
shoulders were the pipes.

"It's the doctor," explained one of the villagers who
was showing us around. "He's our only doctor in these parts.
An' what a mon!"

What a mon indeed! Here was the 51st Highland
Division personified; the Scots in full attack. He came right
up to us, looked me straight in the eye and said: "Has that
man been insulting ye?"

"Forget it," I said.

"Nae," he said. "He's nae guid. He's nae one o' us. His
clan were never no guid!" Then his eyes glazed over and a
smile came out of his bottom jaw. "I'll play ye a tune," he
said. "I'll play ye a piobairachd on the pipes wi' all the
hatred in the world in it!" He spat on the floor.

And as he played this haunting, vital tune that stirred
even the English hearts present, I saw through the pipe-
smoke the desert and the men of Alamein before the attack
that changed the course of the war against Hitler. I dare say
those sturdy, silent Scots who stood around the room saw
even more than that.

I was to learn more about the survival of the clan
tradition on another visit to Scotland when I called at the
offices of the Scots Ancestry Research Society in Edinburgh.
There Isabel Allan was earning dollars for Britain in this
non-profit-making service of tracing the predecessors of Scots
and of those who like to think they have border blood in
their veins.

As I spoke to her, Miss Allan was dealing with an
inquiry from Mr. McCluggage, of Seattle, America. Mr.
McCluggage was anxious to know if he was entitled to wear
the McDougal tartan, and the research had shown that he

was. The news was costing him two dollars; for another four he could learn all about his pedigree.

"Miss Allan," I said, "is there any chance for me? Do the Pickleses hail from Perth, do you think?"

Evidently, Miss Allan thought not; but, for all that, she did a bit of tracing before shaking her head.

"What about Mrs. Pickles?" she asked. I looked at Mabel, and Mabel winked. "Not a hope," she said.

Miss Allan looked interested. "What's your mother's maiden name?"

There was a pause. "Kelly," said Mabel.

What astonished me about this exotic city of Edinburgh was to find such dingy tenements behind the façade of high living standards and glorious architecture and town planning. I was just as appalled at Wester Ross, and in the Highlands generally, to come across so much neglect and so many signs of social backwardness and human poverty. In these magnificent hills of surprising views and fairyland waterfalls, blue space, heather and vintage air, there is little evidence of improvements in the life of the people. I rode along Desolation Way, that road they built for food, the unemployed Highlanders of another age, and thought of the harshness of the lives of those who had struggled, foot by foot, to make this highway north from Inverness through Gairloch, by Gruinnard Bay, along the shore of Little Loch Broom and by Fisherfields Forest.

Puzzled, I wondered what could be done for the folk of Wester Ross, whose livelihood must come from the sea yet who are so ill-served by lines of communication that trade with the world beyond the surrounding hills is uneconomical because of the cost of transporting goods. Something would have to emerge to keep them going; for in our tight-packed island we cannot afford to have whole chunks of our land uninhabited and undeveloped.

Perhaps the most inspiring symbol of hope is the hydro-electric scheme that has made such headway and which offers the prospect of higher standards of life and new ways of making a living for the people who dwell in these hills. Already it has brought electric light to homes in many parts of the spreading Highlands; and I heard of one old cottager who had her "wee butt an' benn" wired up.

A few weeks later, an inspector went round to look at the meter. It registered two units.

"Do ye no use the electric light?" he asked the old lady.

"Oh, aye," she replied. "Every night—to see my way to light the lamps!"

In all my trips through Scotland I have never noticed even a hint of the meanness that is supposed to characterize the Scots. I believe this myth is of their own devising, a trick they play on the rest of us. Once, in Glasgow, I met Henry Hall, and he recalled an occasion when he was appearing at the Empire Theatre there. In the stalls was that grand Scot, Sir Harry Lauder.

"I called him up on the stage," said Henry. "There was terrific applause. It followed him all the way from his seat, along the front aisle, up the steps and right up to the microphone."

Sir Harry held up his hands to quieten the house. Then he looked hard at the audience and said: "An' to think I paid for my seat!"

I believe I would be happy living among the Scots, in whom dourness and excitability are so oddly mingled; for these people have humour; they are down-to-earth, and are justly proud of their heritage and their history in peace and war. I agree with Burns:

> "When o'er life's sea I ferry o'er,
> A time that surely shall come,
> In Heaven itself I'd ask no more
> Then just a Highland welcome."

It was in Kilmarnock that I was a guest of the local Burns Society at their annual dinner. In came the haggis, carried aloft by a girl to the skirl of the pipes. At the end of the meal, the chairman stood up and said: "I'll propose the loyal toast." He held up his glass: "His Majesty the King." To my surprise, I saw that four or five men in a group remained in their seats; and, when it came my turn to speak,

I referred to this and said: "I'm no sloppy sentimentalist, but I was hurt to see that a few people declined to join in the toast." There was silence. "I agree," I went on, "with the spirit of the call for greater freedom for the Scots from Whitehall. In fact, I think you ought to have your own Parliament, like Ulster and the Isle of Man. But I also believe you should pay allegiance to the King."

I had another surprise coming, for the whole gathering, with the exception of the odd men out, rose and cheered. Then they toasted Mabel and me; that is, all but the little group I had spoken about.

I was told afterwards that they were not Nationalists but Communists.

Now, some five hundred miles from the scene of that incident, I took down from the bookcase a catalogue of clans and tartans that always intrigues me. I have a kilt of my own, which I wear when doing *Have a Go!* as Wullie McPickles north of the border, but I have never been able to find it in the catalogue. I was glancing through the coloured pages, when Mabel appeared and looked over my shoulder.

"I know what we'll do this afternoon," she said, obviously inspired by the book. "We'll go to Nathan's and see if your clothes are ready for *Hobson's Choice*."

"I thought we were on holiday?" I said.

"Well, if you don't want to bother!"

"But I do. Let's be off."

What actor could resist a chance to go to Nathan's, that Alice-in-Wonderland corner of the West End, where you can dress up to your heart's delight from a range of costumes that takes in every change of fashion for hundreds of years? This theatrical costumier's shop is a paradise for performers who don't want to live their own lives but somebody else's. I am a fine one to talk, for I know only too well the "fatal fascination of this unreality."

As soon as I was inside the entrance that is for all the world like the door to some Aladdin's cave, the atmosphere of the place gripped me; its smell of unworn cloth and mothballs; the grotesque unreality of the Elizabethan dresses and frilly skirts and suits of armour; the belts and boots and braces, and the straight faces of the actors, producers and tailors in the midst of this surrealist chaos.

A bright young man in a modern Savile Row suit approached us. "We didn't expect you today, sir. But we're ready for you."

He led us upstairs, past groups of ordinary-looking men and women solemnly saying things like: "But this, darling, is the seventeenth century" and "I tell you that when I meet the prince I must be wearing my coronet." We were shown into an anteroom full of colourful period dresses, and in no time at all I was standing in front of a mirror in my underpants, short socks and suspenders, with a billycock on my head. And an elegant young man was saying: "Oh yes, Mr. Pickles, that's 1880 all right. You look wonderful!"

I looked down at my underpants. "What about trousers?" I said. Out they came, tight-legged and narrow at the bottoms, the genuine article; then there appeared the elastic-sided boots, the starched collar, the shoelace tie, black and deplorably unmasculine—and, of course, the cuffs.

"Wear them right round," said the serious young man. "Don't make them oval-shaped." He stood with his chin in his hand watching me parade up and down like somebody who had escaped from my great-grandfather's day. Mabel sat by the window, wondering perhaps whether this little man with the tight-shouldered jacket and drainpipe trousers and little black bowler curved at the edges could really be her husband!

I regarded myself in the tilted mirror. In the background of the reflection was Mabel and the serious-faced assistant, and Mr. Nathan himself, who was looking like an art critic at a preview. For a moment I felt like laughing. Then the mood passed off, and I was once more the man-of-the-theatre who is used to such carryings-on.

I turned to Mabel. "What do you think?"

"It's good. But I'm not sure about that hat."

I tried three other bowlers, but none looked quite as pathetically in character as the original one, so I stuck to that.

As we left Nathan's and drove through Leicester Square,

I wondered what made so many of us want to dress up and play charades and pretend to be other people. Could it be that the world of reality was too grim? Or was it something uncontrollable in our personalities? The psychiatrists, of course, would give me an easy answer full of lessons from apparently innocent childhood experiences. But I was not at all sure that they had the right explanation.

I wondered how many of the hundreds of young people who had written to us asking for advice about stage careers would someday go into Nathan's to try on their theatrical costumes. "I want to go on the stage. . . ." Judging from our mail there are boys and girls in every town and village and suburb in the country who are longing to act professionally. Usually I suggest to them that they should try to get into the Royal Academy of Dramatic Art.

"You know, Mabel," I said, as we made for home, "I've intended for years to see R.A.D.A. at work. We keep saying we'll go and we never do."

"Well, there's not going to be much chance after tomorrow."

Tomorrow! The end of our holiday; and then off on a constant round of travel, interviews, shows and negotiations.

"Do you think they would mind if we went now?"

"Why should they?" Mabel replied.

We made for Gower Street and that modest entrance, tucked away in a street of modern flats and offices, that for so many has been an archway to fame and fortune. Sir Kenneth Barnes, the principal, was out when we arrived, and we were shown over the school by Miss Mary Pilgrim, his secretary.

Everybody knew her, I noticed, and not a single student passed without greeting this energetic woman, who has a great sense of humour and the most down-to-earth approach to the affairs of show business. We went into a poetry-reading class; burst in on a group of students who were involved in an excerpt of high drama, and then slipped into a narrow room where some thirty youngsters were learning poise and the way to walk.

167

Miss Pilgrim looked at her list. "There's a diction class going on under somebody you must know."

"Who's that?" I asked.

"Lionel Marson."

Lionel, away from his B.B.C. news-reading studio, was astonished to find me sitting among his four pupils, one of whom was a shy young boy with one of the finest natural voices I have ever heard. It was here that we were joined by Sir Kenneth, an authoritative figure with grey hair and a slight stoop and a tendency to look at you over his spectacles.

"I know we've nodded to each other on occasions, Pickles, but we've never had the chance to have a proper talk, have we?"

Mabel smiled—and I knew why.

Should I tell the story? I hesitated. Mabel sensed my doubts, nodded approvingly and started turning her wedding ring round and round on her third finger. This is no secret sign or anything like that, but it usually means that she is waiting for me to carry on, and in this case it was clear that she saw no harm in letting Sir Kenneth know that I had once seen him for "a proper talk."

I started to explain. "It was your sister, Sir Kenneth— Dame Irene Vanbrugh—who gave me an introduction to you here in London. I came down to your office——"

"Don't say you tried to get into R.A.D.A.!"

"It was twenty-eight years ago."

"Well I'll be ——! And what happened, do tell me?"

"You told me you might do something for me if I could only get rid of my Yorkshire accent!"

Just for a few seconds Sir Kenneth stood transfixed. Then he came out with a great chuckle and, gazing at Mabel and me over his spectacles, said: "But I didn't turn you down, did I?"

That seemed to be the best ending to the R.A.D.A. incident, and I did not tell our host that the reason I had not taken a course at the Academy he loves was because I had not enough money. Perhaps it was a good thing, for I might have gone and lost what turned out to be my greatest asset.

I feel, however, that young actors and actresses do
benefit from Academy training—so long as they do not
regard their teachers as saints who can do and say no wrong,
and so long as they make up their minds not to absorb that
which they cannot conscientiously accept. There is a great
danger, too, when any art is brought down to classroom
theories, of young people being led into an arty-crafty coterie
of sophisticated cynics. I have seen it happen so often that I
believe Shakespeare's lines about the art of the actor should
be displayed prominently over the doors of every drama
school in the country:

> "To hold, as 'twere, the mirror up to nature,
> To show virtue her own features,
> Scorn her own image,
> And the very age and body of the time his
> form and pressure."

The Academy has produced some brilliant players—
people like Vivien Leigh, Gladys Young, Herbert Lomas
and Richard Attenborough—and in *The Pleasure's Mine*
we introduced to radio a nineteen-year-old girl, only recently
out of the school, who read poetry brilliantly. I mentioned
this to Sir Kenneth, and he agreed with me that Barbara
Jefford is an exceptionally talented actress. Barbara is tall,
dark and attractive, and if her name is not blazing from the
neons of Shaftesbury Avenue in the next few years—well,
I'm a Lancastrian!

While we were having tea in Sir Kenneth's office, I
started making friends with his affectionate, golden-haired
dog.

"I see," he observed, "that you have a nice dog
language, too!" Then he recalled that he used to take the
dog on his weekly visits to George Bernard Shaw. "He was
proud of his dog talk, you know." It was an altogether new
side of the great master's nature that was rather surprising.

The young students were leaving for their homes and
"digs" and attic rooms when Mabel and I came away. We
hailed a passing taxi. The driver knocked his "For Hire" sign

down, tilted an ear into the back, shot a quizzical glance at some students grouped close to the edge of the pavement, and said: "Queer lot o' kids these!" And that was all he did say until we reached the flat.

"One and four to you, Wilf," he grinned as we stepped out.

"Don't spend it all at once," I said, handing him two bob.

"No chance o' that. Stayin' in tonight. But tomorrer! Tomorrer me and the missus goes to the theatre."

"You prefer it to the pictures?" I asked.

"More natural, if you know what I mean. Go every fortnight. Saw a play the other week where they talked just like we do at 'ome."

Then he was off, this taxi-driver who thought the drama students an odd lot; this ordinary theatregoer who had the power to make or break the careers of those youngsters in Gower Street.

I was speculating about the frail line that divides fame and failure for so many artists, when Mabel exclaimed: "Oh, look!"

There, on the landing outside the door of our flat, was a beautiful bunch of flowers. Mabel gently picked it up and searched for the name of the sender. There was no trace. Who could it be? We were left guessing, and tossed names of possible well-wishers across the kitchen table as Mabel put the flowers into a vase. In the end we gave it up. But it was encouraging to know that we had such an anonymous friend.

◘◘

CHAPTER TWELVE

Friday week

OUR TRAVELLING BAGS AND CASES LAY LITTERED ROUND the bedroom, and on the dressing table were two monthly returns from King's Cross to Newcastle. Mabel was holding up a dress with a "shall-I-take-this?" expression on her face. I was by the window, holding a morning paper to the light and pretending to be engrossed in the news. In fact, I was merely reluctant to face the end of our holiday.

"Anything happening?" asked Mabel.

"Usual bother," I replied. "Nobody can seen anybody else's point of view."

"No murders?"

I turned back from the sports page. "No murders," I said.

"Hey, Pickles! Do you want your green tweed suit?"

"Better go in, I suppose."

I stepped over the four pairs of shoes—two of mine, two of Mabel's—that lay between me and the door, and made for the lounge to pick up Phyllis Bentley's latest book and two anthologies of verse that I intended to take to Newcastle.

On the table was the morning's mail, all neatly bundled and stacked ready for opening. We had decided to read and reply to most of the letters while on tour, and to leave the rest until we returned to London; but I could not resist slitting the top few open.

There were the usual messages from listeners congratulating and criticizing me about some programme; one or two brief notes seeking advice about personal problems; and a reply from a gentleman at St. Annes, near Blackpool, to a letter of mine. I remembered that he had written to ask Mabel and me to open a garden party in the town, and, not having noticed the address, I had told my secretary to let him know that, as I was appearing in Blackpool for fifteen weeks, I would not be able to go.

This was the answer I had given to scores of garden-party invitations, which always roll in at the beginning of summer from all parts of Britain. Now he had written: "I don't quite understand. We asked you BECAUSE you will be appearing in Blackpool and will be among us locally for the season!"

I put the letter on one side for immediate attention and picked up an envelope with a Devon postmark. In it were three closely typed pages, and the more I read the more excited I became.

"Mabel," I called, walking towards the door and still reading. "What d'you think about this?" All my forebodings about returning to work fell away; the last-day blues were, for the moment, gone under the impact of a brilliant idea from someone called P. A. Horwill, of Bovey Tracey.

Mabel appeared from the bedroom, wearing a plastic apron over her blouse and grey skirt, and carrying, over one arm, what looked like a stack of my trousers. "Don't tell me," she said with a grin, "that we're not going to Newcastle after all; that we're having another week's holiday?"

"Who wants another week?" I said, waving the letter.

"You did—five minutes ago."

That was true enough, for, from the moment of waking, I had dwelt on the disappearance of twelve days that should have been more lazily spent; I had thought nostalgically of the Friday before—when our holiday was still young—rather as a child does on seeing his parents tying his bucket and spade to the old leather trunk and saying "Thanks for a lovely time" to the landlady.

It was all over bar the packing, and at breakfast Mabel looked at me and said: "You're a fiend for work and you need a lot of stopping—but once you do stop . . . !" I had gone back in retrospect to other holidays, to those escapes from the grinding imprisonment of Halifax in my boyhood, to those migrations from the northern mill towns that had gone on, year in and year out, for longer than I could recall;

to the "wakes," "feasts" and "bowling tides"; to the "rush-bearing" that means the annual holiday in north Yorkshire. Once I had inquired into the origin of "rushbearing" and discovered that it was the custom to organize a week in which the villagers would gather in the rushes to lay on the earthen floor of the church to make it warm for winter. And it was in one of those beautiful little country churches that I had heard them singing this delightful hymn:

"Praise be to God that He has planned
Beneath the sky so good a land,
Bracken on hillside, rocks that gleam,
Greenness and fields beside the stream.

"Waters run down on rainy days
And laugh along ten thousand ways,
Down from the mists where shepherds keep,
High on the fells, lambs and sheep.

"Daily in old time, year by year,
Men went to work from houses here;
Daily returned, like rooks that fly
Home to the wood across the sky.

"Now all their name and place forgot
Their village ways remembered not,
Sorrow and toil for them are done,
Laughter and play beneath the sun.

"Lord, to the place where once they kneeled
We bear green rushes fresh from field,
This is the custom, theirs and ours,
Rushes to bear and crowns of flowers."

What, after all, was a holiday if it was not a free fulfilment of personality? I thought of the boisterous, madcap holidaymakers, full of sunshine spirit, who paraded the promenade at Blackpool singing, laughing and making way for nobody; men and women bursting out from the chains of reality, from the routine of clocking-on, clocking-off, and going for dinner; from the clanging roar of their machines. It was all healthily vulgar, even to the paper hat with "Kiss Me Quick!" and "Are Yer Coortin'?" boldly emblazoned across the front.

I thought, too, of our American holiday, and was seized with a longing to go back to New York and Chicago and Niagara Falls, and to see the sunset in the Rocky Mountains, the majesty of Salt Lake, the awe-inspiring Grand Canyon and the inimitable charm of San Francisco. What a holiday that was! There, when we docked at Pier 90, was the B.B.C. man in New York, Norman Luker, waiting to greet us and see us through the Customs. From that moment our holiday was as hectic as anything Blackpool can offer. I looked up at the Waldorf-Astoria Hotel and recalled Priestley's apt description of this fantastic building—"about the size of Cheltenham, only vertical." Our room was twenty-five floors up and Mabel found it fun to look down on the ant-heap that was life below.

When we awoke on our first morning, having been telephoned by a cheerful female voice, Mabel made for the window and exclaimed: "Come and look. The taxis are like ladybirds!" Even the thought of it made me dizzy. In Chicago they invited me to do a broadcast, and I tried to give listeners an idea of the sort of radio programmes we hear in Britain. As I ended my talk, the compère, a bespectacled man with a tie that looked as if it had been designed by Picasso, came up close and said: "So you don't advertise on your radio?"

"We don't," I said. And then, as a proud afterthought, I added: "Thank goodness."

He promptly thrust the closing "blurb" under my nose. "O.K. Read this!"

I found myself reading, with as much passion as I could muster: "Have you ever tried So-and-so's cooking fat? Believe me, marm, it's wonderful! It's purer, it's more wholesome and it's more economical! Buy a tin today and see that lovely golden brown on those beautiful French fried potatoes. Yes, marm, it's all I say it is and more. Let your watchword always be, 'So-and-so's cooking fat'!" This brought the house down, to say nothing of what it did to my already low opinion of commercial broadcasting—even though I did carry off, as prizes, six white shirts, a gross of razor blades, a pair of cuff-links, a shaving set, lunch at the finest hotel in Chicago, dinner at the best restaurant and a three-hour cruise on Lake Michigan.

All the incidents of that holiday flooded back on me: there was the friendly business man in San Francisco who had been advised of our arrival in his home city by a fellow-American we had met in New York. He sent a huge basket of roses and pink carnations and a Cellophane box containing a spray of orchids. The attached card merely said: "For Mrs. Pickles. Welcome to San Francisco."

Now another more modest holiday was over, and here I was, already concerning myself with a letter that meant serious work. As I started reading it aloud, Mabel beckoned me forward with: "You can read it to me while I'm packing." I followed her, sat on a case she had filled and began:

"Dear Sir,
"Having read that you are seeking a new type of programme for the future, I venture to write to you with a suggestion which perhaps you will consider.

"Outside all questions of religion, the world is divided into two main types of mankind: those who are ruled and those who rule themselves. These two 'black and white' classes are shaded at each end by types who are neither one nor the other.

"We in this country believe that we should rule ourselves, guided by one political belief or another with, I hope, a fair degree of personal disinterest in our outlook. Personally, I find too often that I am too ignorant of the problems of a conflict to carry out my first duty as a citizen, which is to decide where the truth of a dispute lies. Yet if I do not know, I cannot take my share in ruling myself.

"How often can I say who is right, or wrong, in a

175

trade dispute? I still don't know what the dock strike
was about. I still cannot see why 'working to rule' by
the railway workers, or postal workers, can bring such
dislocation, for I cannot see what sense there is in
bringing in a code of rules which are, apparently, only
producers of chaos if obeyed. I can only make my own
guess as to why a nationalised industry never pays—but
I cannot give full weight to the other side of the picture
because I do not know it."

From there, the writer went on to suggest a programme
in which men and women could air their problems and
"moans" and be given a considered reply. I was to "give
coherence" to this parade of public opinion.
"Well," I asked, " what do you think?"
"Sounds good," Mabel replied. "I think it would go
well."
Here was a programme that could contribute vitally to
the British way of life. It seemed to be the essence of what
I had been vaguely looking for to follow *Have a Go!* and it
was certainly in keeping with the spirit and the best
traditions of public-service broadcasting.
I felt fitted to tackle such a programme because of my
own bewilderment about some aspects of public affairs. I was
all for going round to see Kenneth Adam about it right
away, but Mabel counselled otherwise. "Remember," she
said, "you're still on holiday—and we still have the hold-all
and an attaché case to pack."
Over lunch we provisionally christened the programme
that was still no more than an idea. We decided it should be
called *Have a Natter,* and Mabel agreed with me when I said
that ordinary men and women, besides experts, should be
allowed to give their answers to listeners' questions. *Have a
Go!* I knew, had shown how people could enjoy each other's
company and concern themselves with their neighbours'
worries, despite all that was exclusive and isolationist in the
British character.
How often had I sat in train compartments surrounded
by a network of newspapers. Would we ever admit that we

were really, behind the protecting headlines, sociable people? I was reminded of that classic letter which appeared in a newspaper from a man who had found a way to keep other passengers out of his compartment on the eight forty-five. "It is no use talking about fever and measles," he wrote. "This used to work quite satisfactorily, but it does so no longer. The only certain way to get a carriage of my own, I find, is not to stand at the door. I flatten my nose against the window and whenever anybody approaches I beckon them to come in. Nobody does!"

I looked again at the letter from Devon. "Before I conclude," said the writer, "I reserve for myself two income-tax moans. I should enjoy them!" His mention of income tax brought to mind that businesslike Lancastrian, Jack Taylor, one of Blackpool's impresarios, a showman to the fingertips, who on one occasion organized six simultaneous pantomimes. As he had so much money involved he thought it advisable to consult an income-tax inspector about the rewards he might expect from his lavish enterprise.

"Is it," he asked bluntly, "going to be worth my while putting on these shows?"

The official demurred. "It's not for me to say that," he replied with a shrug.

Jack, fresh-complexioned and jovial and a successful practitioner of the how-to-make-friends-and-influence-people technique, rested his arms on the Inland Revenue desk and held his hands upwards appealingly. "Just as a personal opinion, without prejudice to your position," he pleaded. "Tell me!"

"Frankly, Mr. Taylor, it will not be worth it."

Jack grinned. "That's all I wanted to know," he said. "I'm putting them on just the same." In the middle of January a letter arrived at the Inland Revenue office addressed to the inspector.

"Dear Sir," it said, "You will be delighted to hear that all your pantomimes are doing well."

It was men like Jack Taylor who brought prosperity to Blackpool and made it what it is today, the world's greatest resort: a fabulous, fantastic playground, a golden mile of escapism dominated by a tower that concedes nothing to the Eiffel Tower and a pleasure beach that is more varied, more colourful and certainly more original than the much-vaunted Coney Island in America. My mind was filled with pictures of Blackpool and the sounds of its sideshow sensationalists when the telephone rang. It was a gramophone record firm who wanted to make two more discs of popular sing-songs, with me as compère. I had already recorded two in London, and it occurred to me that it might be better to make the next pair elsewhere.

"What about doing them in Blackpool?" I suggested.

Mabel, hearing my voice, came in and stood facing me, with our engagement diary open in her hands. "Let's be sure about our dates," she advised. So often have I made three appointments for the same time that Mabel no longer considers me competent to arrange our diary!

We agreed on a date for the gramophone recording and sat down and glanced through the engagements that lay immediately ahead. I was perched on the arm of the chair, pointing out what gave indications of being rush periods. There were bazaars to open, luncheon meetings to address, radio programmes to record and broadcast, as well as get-togethers with my publisher, my agent, B.B.C. producers and a young film director who had "a really wonderful idea, dear boy!"

I pointed to the entry which said: "Literary luncheon, 1 p.m." "I don't know what I'm going to say there! They will expect a quarter of an hour at least!"

"We'll work something out on the way tonight," said Mabel.

I was reminded of the luncheon given in the Dorchester Hotel by Christina Foyle to launch my autobiography, *Between You and Me*. It was one of the most terrifying moments of my life as I entered the ornate and luxurious room where these bookish operations are organized each month. The hundreds of people sitting at numbered tables seemed to be expecting something superbly witty and extravagantly brilliant; and I felt so impossibly small, especially when I set eyes on the scarlet-jacketed toastmaster, that I wanted to shrink back into the obscurity of Greater London and write nothing more incriminating than anonymous letters to the local papers. The meal was a delight, though I only discovered this long after my ordeal was over. Near us at the long top table was the Bishop of London, an optimistic, amiable man with laughter-wrinkles round his eyes; and Lady Astor, voluble and full of mischievous fun.

When her turn came to speak she immediately leaned into the microphone and, with a piece of subtle leg-pulling, had everybody with her. It was a lesson in public-speaking, the way she collared the audience and had them waiting impatiently on her next words. This magnificent woman with the bubble of youth still in her veins made sharp observations about life and people, and followed them up with a toss of the head that emphasized her mock-indignation.

She took the starch out of the occasion and had us rocking in admiring merriment at her astuteness as she analysed the American accent. This was the main part of her theme, a follow-up to a generous comment on my own news-reading work; and she ended up by gazing first at me and then at the Bishop of London with that stern, no-nonsense expression of hers, and then saying solemnly that she had pleasure in supporting "these goodly, Godly—and entirely mercenary—men!"

I was so impressed and delighted with Lady Astor's personality that I sought her out afterwards. "You were wonderful," I said. "You stole the show."

She stroked her chin, made a gesture of putting one of her grey curls in place, and replied: "I wouldn't do it if I didn't like it." Then, with a reproving twinkle in those eyes, that are at once gay and serious, she said: "They tell me, Pickles, that you have strong views politically?" It was a fair question, so I gave her a straight answer.

"Naturally, I have my views, but I'm not a party man."

Lady Astor wagged a warning finger under my nose. "Don't let them," she said, "don't let them ever make a politician of you. They'll try, you know."

Some months later I had occasion to ring Lady Astor. She was out at the opera and I was told she was not expected back until ten-thirty. At twenty to eleven I called again and her voice boomed over the telephone: "What on earth are you doing up at this time of night?"

Now it was my turn to score off her. "Waiting for you to come in!" I quipped.

It was at another of these book-lunches that I saw as deft an example of public speaking as I am ever likely to come across. Compton Mackenzie, appearing for all the world like the Scarlet Pimpernel in middle age, with his sharp, formidable face and neat goatee beard, and a deceptively light-hearted approach that gave the impression he was out to make a jamboree of the lunch, stood up to speak, grinned sheepishly and then worked himself up into such a verbal frenzy that he completely forgot that Herbert Morrison, the chairman for the occasion, to whom he was proposing a toast, had left early on official business.

With a dramatically searching glance along the table, he set eyes on me and exclaimed: "I know what we'll do! Let's offer a toast to Wilfred Pickles, and I can honestly say I have not missed even one of his *Have a Go!* programmes." It was a delightful tribute that I appreciated all the more because, in such a position, any speaker might easily have been tempted into an offensive remark to pass the buck of embarrassment.

I later found Compton Mackenzie a most entertaining man, rich in humorous anecdotes and faith in ordinary people. In his character there seemed to be all the Frenchman's animation, the fiery stubbornness of the Scot, and none of the archness of the literary set.

Mabel was going through our diary entries with that practised eye which so often detects my administrative failures. "What else were we going to do next week?" she said.

"Looks to be plenty there to go on with," I replied.

"Now what was it?" Mabel paused, then: "I know!" she said.

"Ay!"

"We were going to run through your Willie Mossop lines for *Hobson's Choice.*"

I had forgotten the play. It seemed as if we were back at work with a vengeance. "Do you think we'll ever lead a normal life?" I said. "Will we ever be able to sit back and work regular hours nine to six, and settle down and not have to work, or even think of work, all the time?"

"Now let's not be morbid," quipped Mabel. "Come on, I'll make a cup of tea." I felt better after our "elevenses" and decided to reconcile myself to the fact that for another four months at least there was no chance of another holiday. Down in Devonshire Street life was moving on, much as it had done on the day we had begun our break; there were the usual lines of parked cars, women with poodles and City-dressed men in a hurry.

All over Britain, I thought, men and women would be working their looms, tending their machines, inspecting their fields in the never-ending process of earning the nation's keep. Under the earth in many parts of the land were blackened men hacking out the coal that kept the furnaces going that gave us light, warmth and the power that helped to buy our food and give us the leisure to listen to the radio and watch the shows in which I, and thousands more, played.

It was all relative, and Mayfair and Maesteg seemed close in fact if not in living standards, linked in everything but the philosophy and experiences of their respective populations. There were millions of men, women and children living and working and learning under the sun that now blazed down into our London street; ordinary people with so much in common and yet with so many prejudices and injustices and class divisions and accent barriers to keep them apart. These gulfs widened with neglect; they could not be left to adjust themselves; and just as *Have a Go!* had contributed to understanding and mutual appreciation among folk with different religions, politics, beliefs and occupations, so it seemed that other programmes in the future could do the same, and perhaps more.

I left the window and went into the bedroom where

Mabel was on her knees packing my pyjamas in the little brown suitcase we would keep with us on the sleeper to Newcastle.

"You know, Mabel," I said, "it's not a bad job, is it?"

Mabel snapped the case shut. "There are lots worse." Then she smiled. "I'm rather looking forward to Newcastle, really."

Newcastle! Bracing, crowded and hectic with traffic it would be; and far from the hub of the B.B.C. and the wheels of the entertainment business; an inelegant, hard-working city of lively Geordies; a city like one of the big ships that shelter at its quays—gallant, tough, and full of inspiration for the people within its boundaries. Newcastle! Then Scotland and Cardiff and Lancashire and Blackpool! I wondered whether Mabel would be happier settling down and being a local inhabitant instead of one of the roving kind like me. It was compensating to think that, by the very nature of our work, we could be of real value in bringing folk closer together, in introducing the people to the people. But would either of us find more satisfaction, more personal happiness and sense of fulfilment, if we were to rusticate in a dream house in some favoured spot?

I thought of that delightful northern poem, written by Arthur C. Benson, which Mrs. Hilda Burdock, a London woman now living in Halifax and loving it, had "discovered" for me.

"I would live, if I had my will,
In an old stone grange on a Yorkshire hill,
Ivy-encircled, lichen-streaked,
Low and mullioned, gable-peaked,
With a velvet lawn and a hedge of yew,
An apple orchard to saunter through,
Hyacinth-scented in spring's clear prime
And rich with roses in summer-time,
And a waft of heather over the hill,
Had I my will.

"Over my tree-tops, grave and brown,

182

Friday

Slants the back of a breezy down;
Through my fields, by the covert edge,
A swift stream splashes from ledge to ledge
On to the hamlet, scattered, gray,
Where folk live leisurely day by day;
The same old faces about my walks;
Smiling welcomes and simple talks;
Innocent stories of Jack and Jill;
    Had I my will.

"How my thrushes should pipe ere noon,
Young birds learning the old birds' tune;
Casements wide, when the eve is fair,
To drink the scents of the moonlit air.
Over the valley I'd see the lights
Of the lone hill-farms on the upland heights;
And hear, when the night is alert with rain,
The steady pulse of the labouring train,
With the measured gush of the merry rill,
    Had I my will.

"Then in winter, when gusts pipe thin,
By a clear fire would I sit within,
Warm and dry in the ingle nook,
Reading at ease in a good, grave book;
Under the lamp, as I sideways bend,
I'd scan the face of my well-loved friend;
Writing my verses with careless speed,
One, at least, would be pleased to read;
Thus sweet leisure my days should fill,
    Had I my will.

"Then when the last guest steps to my side—
May it be summer, the windows wide—
I would smile as the parson prayed,
Smile to think I was once afraid;
Death should beckon me, take my hand,
Smile at the door of the silent land,
Then the slumber, how good to sleep

183

Under the grass where the shadows creep,
Where the headstones slant on the wind-swept hill!
    I shall have my will!"

King's Cross was smelly, sooty and shadowed with lonely
travellers when we arrived. The wide stone approach was
packed with trucks loaded with the morning newspapers,
and in the dim half-light I noticed a tired group of
uniformed men, noisy with the language of night. The Newcastle train was already in, with its impatient locomotive and
fussing porters and intimate farewells. As the attendant
showed us to our sleeper I thought of that wartime night
when Mabel and I had to share a sleeper with two young
members of the W.A.A.F. I got a top bunk and hardly dared
move all night!

I recalled this to amuse the attendant who pushed our
bags in after us.

"Bit of an embarrassing moment!" he grinned.

I thought of that other attendant who, a few weeks
earlier, had shown Lionel Gamlin, the B.B.C. compère, to
his sleeper. Looking down the list, the attendant exclaimed:
"Are you Lionel Gamlin of the radio?"

The man inspected him from head to toe and said, with
a sigh of disillusion: "Ay! I 'ad Wilfred Pickles on this
train three months ago. He's not much to look at,
either!"

Mabel sat on her bunk and unlocked the suitcase. Out
came the pyjamas and toothpaste. I noted the washbasin, the
drinking glass, the shelf for morning tea and the hook for
hanging our watches; then I tested the dimmer switch for the
bedside lights.

"Everything all right?" Mabel was already taking her
shoes off. I reached for the hatbox that has not held headgear for years and took from it a half-bottle of whisky and
two glasses.

"Here's to—well, here's to whatever is ahead!"

Just as we held up our glasses the train rattled and
rocked across some violent points and threw us both
sideways.

Friday

"What a life!" said Mabel.

"Oh, to live like normal folk!"

"When's that going to be, Pickles?"

I folded my trousers over the coathanger and undid my cuff-links. "You never know," I said. "This year, next year. . . ."

The End

Index

Index

Index

Index

Index

Richards, Gordon, 102, 105
Richmond, Yorkshire, 98
Riley's billiards tables, 124
Rishton, 69
Rocky Mountains, the, 174
Roger (*Author's dog*), 40
Rome, 29
Rose Marie, 36
Royal Academy of Dramatic Art, 90, 167-9
Royal Air Force, 150
Royal Family, the, 58
Royal Navy, the, 150
"Rushbearing," 173

St. Albans, 122
St. Annes, Lancashire, 171
St. Dunstan's Club, 53
St. Stephen's Hall, 67
Sales, women's, 43
Salt Lake, 174
San Francisco, 101, 174
Sauchiehall Street, Glasgow, 99
Savage Club, the, 89, 152
Scotland, 161, 164
Scots Ancestry Research Society, the, 162
Seattle, U.S.A., 162
"Seasons, The," by John Clare, 13
"Secrets of Freemasonry," 53
Selfridges, Ltd., 26
Shaftesbury Avenue, 169
Shakespeare, William, 24, 27, 28, 29, 115, 169
Shakespeare Memorial Theatre, Stratford-on-Avon, 27, 29
Shakespearian companies, 26, 27, 90, 132
Sharpe, Dolly, 21
Shaw, George Bernard, 22, 104, 105-6, 169
Shaw, Lancashire, 92
Shawcross, R. W., 159
Sheffield, 65, 116
Shelley, Norman, 90
Shelley, Percy Bysshe, and his Harriet, 14
Sheppard, W. V., 144-6, 150
Shirley, by Charlotte Brontë, 22
"Shropshire Lad, A," 20
Sim, Alastair, 63, 90
Simon of Wythenshawe, Lord, 158

Smithfield Market, 150
Snagge, John, 54-5
Sowerby Bridge, 18, 99
Stead, Bob, 113
Stephenson, Donald, 113, 116, 120, 123
Stockholm, 33
Stony Stratford, 97
Stratford-on-Avon, 24-9, 34-7
Sullivan, Mrs. (*of Oswaldtwistle*), 35-7
Swallow, Norman, 47, 116
Swan & Edgar, 135
Swedes, the, 33
Switzerland, 117-9

Take It From Here, 93
"Tam o' Shanter," by Robert Burns, 40-1
Tamworth, 98, 100
Taplin, Lola, 38
Tatler, The, 118
Taxicabs, 51, 53
Taylor, Jack, 177
Tchaikowsky's "Pathétique" Symphony, 28
Tearle, Godfrey, 27, 90
Television, 46, 76, 92, 123, 128, 130
"Templegate" (racing correspondent of *Daily Herald*), 148
Tennent, H. M., Ltd. 11
Tennyson, Alfred, Lord, 50
Territorial Army, the, 65
Thames, River, 70
Theaker, Dinah, 131
These Names Make News (newspaper feature), 59
Thompson, Francis, 28
Thompson, Tommy, 82-5, 93, 96, 116, 121
  his death, 81
  his funeral, 85, 109, 112-6
Thorpe Arch, Yorkshire, 126, 136-8
Tomlinson, George, M.P., 69
Tottington, 114
Tower of London, the, 70
Towers, Harry Alan, 91
Trafalgar Square, 67
Train, Jack, 91
Trio (Somerset Maugham film), 37
Tunstall, 65

Turk's Head Inn, Sowerby Bridge, 18
2 ZY (Manchester Broadcasting Station), 18
Tyneside, 65
Tynesiders, 87, 88

Under the Barber's Pole (B.B.C. programme), 81, 82
Underground Railway, the, 48
United Nations, the, 58, 68

Vanbrugh, Dame Irene, 168
Victoria Hall, Halifax, 19
Victoria Station, 48
Voss, Norway, 31, 33

Wagstaffe, Harold, 131
Waldorf-Astoria Hotel, the, 174
Wales, South, 63, 65, 143
Wallasey, 62
Waller, Jack, 18
Wand, Dr., Bishop of London, 179
Warrington, 84, 104
Warwick, 38
Warwickshire, 29, 37
Washington, Harriet, 92
Watling Street, 98, 100
Wayne, Naunton, 54
Weber, 39
Weedon, 98, 99, 100
Weir, Molly, 94

Wengen, Switzerland, 117-9
West Bromwich, 129
West End, the, 48, 92, 111, 128, 129, 165
Wester Ross, 161-2, 163
Westminster Abbey, 18
What's Funny—And Why, 73
Whitehall, 67, 165
Who's Who, 88
Wilson, Harold, M.P., 67-9
Wilton, Robb, 74-5
Wolsey, Cardinal, 64
Woman's Hour (broadcasting (programme), 40
Wood (*Yorkshire wicketkeeper*), 54-5
Wood, Matthew, 64
Wooland, Norman, 90
Woolworth, F. W. & Co., Ltd., 26, 52
Wordsworth, William, 28, 101-2
Wrigley, Ammon, 28
Wynyard, Diana, 27

Yarmouth, 64
Yeats, William Butler, 28
Yorkshire, 97, 99, 123, 159
Yorkshire accent, 168
Yorkshire Cricket Club, 54
Yorkshire Dales, the, 65, 142
Yorkshire Evening News, 158, 159
"Yorkshire's Five," 142
Yorkshiremen, 124
Young, Gladys, 169